A N
UNCOMPROMISING
LIFE

BY

JOHN MACARTHUR

SCAN THIS CODE WITH YOUR SMARTPHONE
OR OTHER DEVICE TO FOLLOW
ALONG WITH THE SERMON AUDIO.

ISBN: 978-1-955292-06-1

Printed in the United States of America

Valencia, California

CONTENTS

AN UNCOMPROMISING
LIFE

INTRODUCTION

The first nine verses of Daniel 1 introduce us to the portrait of an uncompromising life by filling in the landscape. "In the third year of the reign of Jehoiakim king of Judah, Nebuchadnezzar king of Babylon came to Jerusalem and besieged it. The Lord gave Jehoiakim king of Judah into his hand, along with some of the vessels of the house of God; and he brought them to the land of Shinar, to the house of his god, and he brought the vessels into the treasury of his god. Then the king ordered Ashpenaz, the chief of his officials, to bring in some of the sons of Israel, including some of the royal family and of the nobles, youths in whom was no defect, who were good-looking, showing intelligence in every branch of wisdom, endowed with understanding and discerning knowledge, and who had ability for serving in the king's court; and he ordered him to teach them the literature and language of the Chaldeans. The king appointed for them a daily ration from the king's choice food and from the wine which he drank, and appointed that they should be educated three years, at the end of which they were to enter the king's personal service. Now among them from the sons of Judah were Daniel, Hananiah, Mishael and Azariah. Then the commander of the officials assigned new names to them; and to Daniel he assigned the name Belteshazzar, to Hananiah Shadrach, to Mishael Meshach and to Azariah Abednego. But Daniel made up his mind that he would not defile himself with the king's choice food or with the wine which he drank; so he sought permission from the commander of the officials that he might not defile himself. Now God granted Daniel favor and compassion in the sight of the commander of the officials."

A. Society's Compromise

1. Expressed

Ours is an era of compromise. Most of us learn the art of compromise very early, then simply follow the path of least resistance throughout our lives. If we can get by with a little less than our best, with cheating on the principles we claim to follow, we'll do it. We hold a conviction until it gets in the way; we keep a standard as long as it doesn't infringe on something we want.

Frankly, expedience is the ruling standard of human life; we worship the great god *pragmatism*. Mankind's motto could well be, "If it works for you, do it." Society has abandoned seemingly all moral standards, particularly biblical ones. Our world evidences little conscience, guilt, or remorse.

Politicians who campaign on high standards readily compromise them once in office. We find the same principle in business, from the corporate suite down to the salespeople. Lawyers, rather than serving as society's conscience, compromise their own consciences to win a case. Leaders in all walks of life do likewise. Individually, we learn to lie, cheat, steal, and shade the truth, doing whatever is necessary to get what we want, so that compromise becomes a way of life.

2. Emulated

As believers, we might back down in a confrontation to avoid offending someone or seeming obtrusive. Compromise in the Christian life may be most obvious in the moments you know you should speak of Christ, but you don't.

In fact, the church has compromised with the world so repeatedly, we may not even recognize what those compromises are anymore. Whenever the world invents something new, the church invariably follows along—if the world has a hippie movement, we have a Jesus-hippie movement. If the world goes for rock music or women's liberation, so do we.

We have so long compromised with the world and become so engulfed in its materialistic, stylistic value systems that we can barely comprehend an uncompromising life. We fight to be separated from the world, yet we're unable to define what that separation means because we're so brainwashed into accepting and indulging the world's thought patterns and behaviors. Even when we know the Bible prohibits a certain activity, we often do it anyway.

A couple who wanted to be married came in for counseling. But after finding no biblical justification for their marriage, we counseled them that they had no grounds to proceed. They simply went down the street and got married, then showed up at our church again the next week. When we compromise, we substitute ourselves in the place of God.

B. Scripture's Call

In contrast, from one end of the Bible to the other, God clearly commands His people to live apart from the world.

1. The call established

When God established Israel, He built the principle of separation from the world into the Israelites' daily living through how they dressed, ate, and conducted themselves. Their religious observances throughout the year safeguarded them as a unique people (Deut. 14:2), preventing them from intermingling with surrounding pagans.

In the New Testament also, God calls all of His people to be holy and distinct from the world (1 Pet. 2:9). Second Corinthians 6:17–18 summarizes the New Testament's teaching on this: "'Therefore, come out from their midst and be separate,' says the Lord. 'And do not touch what is unclean; and I will welcome you. And I will be a father to you, and you shall be sons and daughters to Me,' says the Lord Almighty." God is uncompromisingly holy, and He instructs His people to show that they are His by refusing to compromise in holiness too.

2. The consequences explained

When Christians compromise with the world, it devastates two primary areas:

a. Compromise destroys our worship

1) Hebrews 13:12–15—"Therefore Jesus also, that He might sanctify ["set apart," or "separate"] the people through His own blood, suffered outside the gate" (v.

12). When it was time for Israel to slay the lamb for the people's sins, those sins were symbolically placed upon another animal that was then taken outside the city, symbolically separating the sins from the people. Likewise, Jesus died outside the city walls, separated from human society. "So, let us go out to Him outside the camp, bearing His reproach" (v. 13)—let's follow Christ and be separate—"For here we do not have a lasting city, but we are seeking the city which is to come. Through Him then, let us continually offer up a sacrifice of praise to God, that is, the fruit of lips that give thanks to His name" (vv. 14–15). You cannot worship unless you are separate. Don't come to God with your praise, thanksgiving, and good deeds unless you've obeyed His call to first come out of the world and be set apart for God.

2) 1 John 2:15—"Do not love the world nor the things in the world. If anyone loves the world, the love of the Father is not in him."

3) James 4:4—"You adulteresses, do you not know that friendship with the world is hostility toward God? Therefore whoever wishes to be a friend of the world makes himself an enemy of God."

b. Compromise destroys our service

Compromise makes us useless. Second Timothy 2:20 says, "Now in a large house there are not only gold and silver vessels, but also vessels of wood and of earthenware, and some to honor and some to dishonor." In God's church, there are containers or utensils (Gk., *skeuos*) of honor and dishonor. To be a utensil God takes pleasure in using, you must cleanse yourself (v. 21) from false teachers and false standards of living (vv. 14–18). You must "abstain from wickedness" (v. 19), "flee from youthful lusts" (v. 22), and "refuse foolish and ignorant speculations, knowing that they produce quarrels" (v. 23). Only then can you be "a vessel for honor, sanctified, useful to the Master, prepared for every good work" (v. 21).

Failure to be separate unto God destroys our worship and service to Him. And sometimes the purging and purification that separation requires means taking drastic steps.

3. The commitment exemplified

Scripture records key individuals who exemplified the holy life God calls His people to.

a. Hebrews 7:26 says of our Lord, "It was fitting for us to have such a high priest, holy, innocent, undefiled, separated from sinners." Jesus Christ is the ultimate pattern for the life of holy commitment.

b. Hebrews 11:25–27 says of Moses, "Choosing rather to endure ill-treatment with the people of God than to enjoy the passing pleasures of sin, considering the reproach of Christ greater riches than the treasures of Egypt; for he was looking to the reward. By faith he left Egypt, not fearing the wrath of the king; for he endured, as seeing Him who is unseen." Moses chose God and heaven over Pharaoh and the earth. He chose affliction in God's will over Egypt's riches outside of God's will.

c. Ruth made a similar commitment: "[Naomi] said, 'Behold, your sister-in-law has gone back to her people and her gods; return after your sister-in-law.' But Ruth said, 'Do not urge me to leave you or turn back from following you; for where you go, I will go, and where you lodge, I will lodge. Your people shall be my people, and your God, my God. Where you die, I will die, and there I will be buried. Thus may the Lord do to me, and worse, if anything but death parts you and me'" (Ruth 1:15–17). Naomi told Ruth to return to her former Moabite life and its idols, but Ruth refused; she was committed to God, and to Naomi as His representative.

d. David wrote, "I have sworn and I will confirm it, that I will keep Your righteous ordinances.

Depart from me, evildoers, that I may observe the commandments of my God" (Ps. 119:106, 115).

e. Acts 11:23 says of Barnabas, the man of God so instrumental in the early church, "When he arrived and witnessed the grace of God, he rejoiced and began to encourage them all with resolute heart to remain true to the Lord." Barnabas told the early church to uncompromisingly cling to the Lord.

f. But no one better exemplifies the character of an uncompromising spirit than Daniel. In fact Ezekiel, a contemporary of Daniel's, listed history's great men of righteousness as "Noah, Daniel and Job" (14:14); he honored Daniel alongside the other two, though they were long dead and Daniel still lived. Let's examine why this truly exceptional man merited that honor.

LESSON

I. THE PLIGHT (DAN. 1:1–2)

"In the third year of the reign of Jehoiakim king of Judah, Nebuchadnezzar king of Babylon came to Jerusalem and besieged it. The Lord gave Jehoiakim king of Judah into his hand, along with some of the vessels of the house of God; and he brought them to the land of Shinar, to the house of his god, and he brought the vessels into the treasury of his god."

A. Jerusalem Besieged (v. 1)

The book of Daniel begins on a sorrowful note by recounting the first stage of Israel's Babylonian captivity. The Northern Kingdom had been taken away long ago; judgment then arrived for the Southern Kingdom, Judah, for its own unfaithfulness and disobedience to God. Nebuchadnezzar essentially ruled the known world in ruling Babylon. He besieged Jerusalem and removed some of its inhabitants in a series of three deportations, the first occurring in Jehoiakim's time in 605 BC.

B. Judah Warned (v. 2)

God didn't judge His people without first warning them. The prophets had constantly reminded the nation of inevitable judgment if they didn't repent. Also, God had allowed the Assyrians to invade Israel, giving His people a preview of foreign oppression. Finally, He made an example of the Northern Kingdom by taking them into captivity for their transgressions. But Judah ignored all of those warnings and continued in their sin. God was patient, merciful, and gracious with them, but as He said in Genesis 6:3, "My Spirit shall not strive with man forever."

C. Daniel Deported

Daniel, his friends, and other young men were taken in the first Babylonian deportation. God was establishing Daniel in the foreign kingdom before the rest of captive Israel arrived.

D. Nebuchadnezzar Triumphant

Nebuchadnezzar did not dethrone Jehoiakim, king of Judah, after besieging and defeating him. Knowing he had been a willing vassal to Egypt in the past, Nebuchadnezzar saw Jehoiakim's weakness and left him in place.

To loot the treasures of foreign gods was proof of the conqueror's greatness and of that god's powerlessness, so it was a common practice for bolstering national wealth and prestige (cf. 1 Sam. 5:1–2). Nebuchadnezzar took everything of value from the Temple. He transferred them to the house of his god, Bel (also called Baal, Merodach, and Marduk). God likely ordained that this incident be recorded to show how comprehensive the coming doom would be: God allowed His own Temple to be robbed. He was no longer defending Judah.

These were hard times for Daniel. Even seventy years after his deportation, he faithfully prayed (cf. 6:10) and obviously longed for Jerusalem—we can only imagine what filled his heart when the city first fell.

II. THE PLOT (DAN. 1:3–7)

The historical background of this passage sets the stage for all of Daniel's life in Babylon. As Nebuchadnezzar was besieging Jerusalem, he received word of his father's death. So he returned to Babylon to assume the throne, leaving Jehoiakim on Judah's throne. Thus the first deportation was not a mass removal of people; Nebuchadnezzar simply took hostages with him to keep Judah in line until he could return and complete his conquest.

A. Taking the hostages (vv. 3–4)

"Then the king ordered Ashpenaz, the chief of his officials, to bring in some of the sons of Israel, including some of the royal family and of the nobles, youths in whom was no defect, who were good-looking, showing intelligence in every branch of wisdom, endowed with understanding and discerning knowledge, and who had ability for serving in the king's court . . ."

1. The chief official (v. 3)

Nebuchadnezzar commanded Ashpenaz to take hostages from Judah's princely nobility. Ashpenaz—either a proper name or a title for one who is an overseer—was "the master [or "prince"] of [Nebuchadnezzar's] eunuchs" (vv. 7–8, NKJV).

Isaiah identifies a eunuch as "a dry tree"

(56:3). Historically, some kings had surgically emasculated servants oversee their harems. Because of that association with courtly service, the term *eunuch* eventually applied to many who served the king but who were not necessarily physical eunuchs. Genesis 39:1 uses the Hebrew word for *eunuch* when introducing Potiphar, though he was married (v. 7). However, Daniel may have been a literal eunuch by the king's command, upon entering his service. That could explain why Daniel, who was never identified with a wife or a family, served these foreign kings for the rest of his life.

2. The children of Israel (vv. 3–4)

Some historians indicate that somewhere between fifty and seventy-five hostages were taken. "Of the sons of Israel" (v. 3) does not mean they were from the Northern Kingdom rather than the Southern Kingdom of Judah; Assyrian invasions in the north had forced a migration of the remnant of the tribes into Judah, so these southern hostages were "of the royal family and of the nobles" (v. 3).

Nebuchadnezzar intended to make Judah a vassal state. He had a detailed plan to retrain his young Israelite hostages in courtly Chaldean ways so they could administer his rule among the Jews. The Babylonians selected their captives by specific criteria.

a. Physical qualities (v. 4)

   1) Age

      ". . . youths . . ."

      Most commentators agree that the youths (Heb., *yeledim*) were no older than seventeen and no younger than thirteen or fourteen. Daniel was a teenager at this time, possibly just fourteen or fifteen years old.

   2) Appearance

      ". . . in whom was no defect, who were good-looking . . ."

      Nebuchadnezzar wanted healthy, physically flawless youths. "Defect" (Heb., *mum*) refers to a physical blemish; "good-looking" emphasizes appearance, particularly of the face. This is typical—Israel, too, chose Saul to be king based on his outward characteristics.

b. Mental qualities (v. 4)

   1) " . . . showing intelligence in every branch of wisdom . . ."

      The youths were also to be intellectually superior, able to make distinctions and decisions and to apply truth practically.

   2) " . . . endowed with understanding . . ."

They were to have received an elite education. The literal translation from Hebrew is "knowers of knowledge"; they were to be good students who had received the right information.

3) ". . . and discerning knowledge . . ."

This Hebrew phrase carries the idea of being able to correlate facts, to harmonize information in order to make wise decisions. It speaks to a scientific ability to collect data and then draw conclusions from it.

c. Social qualities (v. 4)

". . . and who had ability for serving in the king's court . . ."

Finally, Nebuchadnezzar also sought specific social qualities in his captives: the poise, manners, and social graces necessary to stand in a king's court.

The world evaluates people on their physical, mental, and social qualities. The Babylonians had little concern for character or spirituality, virtue or morality. They simply sought the smartest, best-looking, most polished young Jews to remake in their own image.

B. Training the hostages (vv. 4–7)

1. Reeducation (v. 4)

". . . and he ordered him to teach them the literature and language of the Chaldeans."

Originally, the Chaldeans were a separate people, but the Babylonian Empire grew so dominated by Chaldean astrology, sciences, and other disciplines that *Chaldean* and *Babylonian* came to be used interchangeably. The plan was to reform the noble Jewish captives into full-fledged Babylonians through Chaldean education.

a. Languages

The powerful and important language of that day was Chaldean. The Jews would have had to learn it to effectively communicate in their new environment. *The International Standard Bible Encyclopedia* says, "the learning of the Chaldeans . . . comprised the old languages of Babylonia (the two dialects of Sumerian, with a certain knowledge of Kassite, which seems to have been allied to the Hittite; and other languages of the immediate neighborhood)" ([Chicago: Howard-Severance, 1925], 591). These Jewish youths were to become linguistic experts.

b. Literature and sciences

The encyclopedia says that Chaldean education also included "knowledge of astronomy and astrology; mathematics, which their sexagesimal system of numeration seems to have facilitated; and a certain amount of natural history . . . . To this must be added a store of mythological learning, including legends of the Creation [and] the Flood [and their extensive pantheon of deities] . . . . They had likewise a good knowledge of agriculture, and were no mean architects, as the many celebrated buildings of Babylon show" (591). Babylon's famous Hanging Gardens married a number of those disciplines and were one of the seven wonders of the ancient world.

ARE YOUNG PEOPLE BEING BRAINWASHED?

The Babylonians' reeducation efforts are not unlike what many schools and universities attempt on young people today: to undermine their faith and heritage, and replace those with godless, worldly wisdom. Even some seminaries that once upheld the Word of God have abandoned its authority. From the time young people go to school, many teachers present them with a humanistic and atheistic system of values. These values are designed by Satan to undermine the truth of God's Word.

Moses "was educated in all the learning of the Egyptians" (Acts 7:22), but like Daniel, he remained faithful to God. They each refused to forget the truth, so they were able to resist the satanic values they were taught by the erudite educational systems of their day.

---

2. Acculturation (vv. 5–7)

a. Obligation for the future (v. 5)

1) The king's delicacies

"The king appointed for them a daily ration from the king's choice food and from the wine which he drank . . ."

The king's food and wine would have been the finest available. One of the most basic elements in brainwashing is creating a sense of obligation—the Babylonians shrewdly exploited their captives' appetites to build into them a dependency on their lavish provisions. The young men would continue to receive those luxuries only if they served Nebuchadnezzar well.

2) The king's appointments

". . . and appointed that they should be educated three years, at the end of which they were to enter the king's personal service."

That final phrase shows that personal service was the goal of Nebuchadnezzar's conditioning process. Literally translated, the phrase is "stand before," as of angels in God's presence who await a commission to serve (Luke 1:19), or Jeremiah the prophet when he was commissioned to speak to Judah (Jer. 15:19). Nebuchadnezzar intended that after three years of his court's delicacies, the captives would serve him out of obligation—to maintain their luxurious standard of living, and perhaps even from some gratitude for it.

If you've ever tasted a life beyond your own, perhaps you understand that temptation. Few will resist the world's efforts to shape them.

b. Obliteration of the past (vv. 6–7)

Out of all the hostages, apparently only four didn't yield: "Now among them from the sons of Judah were Daniel, Hananiah, Mishael and Azariah. Then the commander of the officials assigned new names to them; and to Daniel he assigned the name Belteshazzar, to Hananiah Shadrach, to Mishael Meshach and to Azariah Abed-nego." In a further effort to make the hostages forget their Hebrew identity, the Babylonians called them by Chaldean names.

This ploy to cut people off from their heritage

is nothing new. Joseph's name was changed in Egypt to Zaphenath-paneah (Gen. 41:45). Esther's true name was Hadassah, but she too was subject to another society and culture (Esther 2:7). Daniel's name, which means "God is judge," was changed to Belteshazzar, which means "Bel provides" or "Bel's prince"; they broke his name's association with God to link him instead with Baal. Likewise, Hananiah ("the Lord is gracious") was dubbed Shadrach, and Mishael ("who is like God?") was altered to Meshach, in order to exalt another chief Babylonian deity. Finally, Azariah ("the Lord is my helper") received the name Abed-nego ("the servant of Nebo") in honor of the son of Baal.

Only a remnant of the faithful existed in Judah by that time, and each of these four Hebrew names reflects the likelihood that these four young men had godly upbringings. That, too, may have distinguished them among the rest of the captives.

In every way, the Babylonians attempted to substitute their demonic pantheon for God.

III. THE PURPOSE (DAN. 1:8a)

"But Daniel made up his mind that he would not defile himself with the king's choice food or with the wine which he drank . . ."

Here is the key to an uncompromising life. Despite the fact that Daniel was only about fourteen years old, he "made up his mind [lit., "laid upon his heart"]" to abstain from the Babylonians' dietary conditioning.

A. The Acceptance

Recall that the effort to reshape the young Israelites took on three distinct fronts: They were to be taught human wisdom, they were to be given heathen names, and they were to be fed heathen food. Daniel and his friends accepted only the first two.

1. Heathen education

Babylonian education was not entirely evil. Daniel and his friends learned many helpful principles of architecture and science.

We'll face moments in our own lives where we must undergo secular training, and the key is to exercise discernment to sort the good from the bad, the true from the false.

2. Heathen names

No name change could affect the fact that their names were written in God's book as His children; nor could it change their hearts.

B. The Abstinence

Daniel drew the line at defiling—polluting or staining—himself with the king's food and wine. But of the three major means of Babylonian integration, why did he object to this one? Wouldn't education have been more crucial?

Daniel's decision was not merely pragmatic. Whereas Scripture did not prohibit taking a heathen name or course of study, it strictly prescribed what a Jew could eat and drink. Daniel exhibited the primary characteristic of an uncompromising life: total commitment to obey the Word of God.

1. Jewish dietary laws

The king's food did not conform to biblical dietary laws. In fact, the Babylonians feasted on delicacies forbidden to Jews, such as pork (Lev. 11). This illustrates part of God's purpose in giving Israel those laws: to restrict them from intermingling with their pagan neighbors.

2. Pagan idolatrous customs

The Old Testament also repeatedly commanded Israel not to tolerate or associate with idolatry of any kind (e.g., Deut. 7). Everything served at the king's table was offered first to Babylonian gods, so to partake of that food was to participate in paganism. Daniel and his friends took their stand on obeying Scripture's clear, specific mandate— that is the character of an uncompromising life.

CONCLUSION

A. The Reasons to Compromise

Daniel had every reason to compromise. He was very young and on his own, away from home and careful parental oversight. Furthermore, having been taught to obey authority and perhaps fearing the temperamental king (cf. Dan. 3:19–20), Daniel may have felt obligated to accept his captors' rules and provisions. Also, if he was ambitious, his advancement in the kingdom demanded unwavering obedience to the king. Finally, Daniel could have believed that God had entirely abandoned Israel in their captivity and been tempted to abandon Him in return.

B. The Refusal to Compromise

What kept Daniel from compromise was his character of integrity. He accepted his captors' education and his new name, but he never accepted their lifestyle. And in his refusal, Daniel wasn't angry or bitter; verse 9 says that "God granted Daniel favor and compassion in the sight of the commander of the officials." The character of an uncompromising life is absolute obedience to God's Word and its principles, lived out in love. When you live an uncompromising life, you will be useful to God.

FOCUSING ON THE FACTS

1. What tempts Christians to compromise? Connect your answer to our ability to perceive compromise. When we compromise, what are we truly doing?

2. What standard does God call His people to? How does our failure to live by that standard affect our life in Christ? What can we do to counteract that?

3. Why did Nebuchadnezzar take the Temple treasures? Why did he take hostages?

4. Explain the Babylonians' methods for conditioning their captives. Why was the king's food such an important factor in that? Explain why it also became the factor that Daniel and his friends staunchly rejected, and how this demonstrates the character of an uncompromising life.

5. What were Daniel's strong inducements to compromise? How did he demonstrate strength of godly character in refusing to do so?

PONDERING THE PRINCIPLES

1. Judah received more than adequate warning that their indifference to God's commands as well as their injustice and unrighteousness would yield judgment (cf. Isa. 5:1–7). Think of a time it took you multiple warnings from God's Word and Holy Spirit to "get the message." Why didn't you respond immediately? What finally got your attention? How has God's loving discipline strengthened you against that particular area of disobedience? Thank God for His abundant grace and patience as He transforms us from those who pursue youthful lusts to those who desire righteousness from pure hearts (2 Tim. 2:22).

2. Have you ever permanently "borrowed" something from work because they "owed" you? Have you disregarded a law because you were in a hurry or because no one would get hurt? Do you profess to honor marriage and family, yet believe and do things that pull them apart? Think of specific times you compromised; what was your foundational motivation in those moments? Did you believe that keeping a certain principle would cheat you of some perceived good? Or that God wasn't concerned or wasn't able to meet the real need at hand? Was it an attempt to speed up God's schedule because you wanted an immediate solution? Read Genesis 15:1–6 and 16:1–6. How did Abraham and Sarah compromise? What was one consequence of their shortcut (16:12; cf. Ps. 83:1–6)? Compare

Abraham's response there with Genesis 22:1–18 (cf. Heb. 11:17–19). Consider your own character today, and whether Scripture would deem it uncompromising. Also, honestly examine how your compromise has hindered your worship and service to God. Review Hebrews 13:12–15, 1 John 2:15, and James 4:4, and memorize whichever passage you are least familiar with. In Christ, you have the divine power you need to depart from evil (cf. 1 John 5:4).

3. Paul tells Christians to "walk as children of Light . . . trying to learn what is pleasing to the Lord" (Eph. 5:8, 10). Such learning should be the believer's continual process. So what are some ways you are learning to please the Lord? How can you be certain what pleases or displeases Him? Memorize these verses from Ephesians to strengthen you against the next time you are tempted to compromise.

4. As Christians, our zeal for God may make us think it's better not to "defile" ourselves by intermingling with nonbelievers. You may also find that your life is essentially contained in Christian circles. Explain the principle expressed in 1 Corinthians 5:9–11. Do your unsaved neighbors ever see you for longer than it takes to pull in or out of your garage? Do your coworkers know what makes you tick? How are you being salt and light to the unbelievers God has placed in your life (Matt. 5:13)? How are you following Daniel's example of doing that with love (Dan. 1:8–9)?

THE CONSEQUENCES OF AN UNCOMPROMISING LIFE,

PART 1

REVIEW

It's astonishing what the person firmly rooted in God can withstand. In life we'll encounter some "gray areas," but on everything about which the Bible gives a specific command, we must take our stand and never compromise. That kind of conviction characterized Daniel's life; his steady hold on the absolutes of God's Word anchored him through the significant storms he faced. Of all the Jewish young men deported in 606 BC, only Daniel and his three friends were able to resist the Babylonians' determined reconditioning.

DANIEL'S PLIGHT
IN OUR DAY

Committed believers today still often face Daniel's plight: If our commitment to God's Word is strong, though we're educated in the world's universities, we can see the weakness of their theories and theology and even bring the truth of the Word back to them. I think of men like Francis Schaeffer who, in many ways, are God's gift to this age—of his diligent study of the world's philosophies so that he could engage them on their own ground with the truth of God. I think also of scientists who have done the same in their own field, and of the godly people who have studied cults and false religions in order to equip us to bring the gospel to the people trapped in those systems of lies.

But if you're unable to implement the same biblical grid Daniel and his three friends used, exposure to worldly education may shipwreck your faith (cf. 1 Tim. 1:19). Not all Christians should expose themselves to the ideologies of secular universities.

LESSON

Having seen the commitment that characterized Daniel's uncompromising life, we'll now examine its consequences. From his policies, it's clear that Nebuchadnezzar was a shrewd and ruthless ruler. He and his successors could also be reckless in retaliation, as the later episodes with the fiery furnace (Dan. 3:16–18, 20) and the lions' den (6:16) show. The price for taking an uncompromising stand can be severe. But Daniel and his friends Hananiah, Mishael, and Azariah were prepared to meet those consequences because of their uncompromising character.

This passage shows us the characteristics of the one who refuses ungodly compromise, even in a godless society.

I. AN UNASHAMED BOLDNESS (DAN. 1:8)

A. Illustrated in the Life of Daniel

"But Daniel made up his mind that he would not defile himself with the king's choice food or with the wine which he drank; so he sought permission from the commander of the officials [Ashpenaz] that he might not defile himself."

In an example of unashamed boldness, Daniel communicated his intention to refrain from the king's food and drink because they would defile him.

WHAT'S YOUR EXCUSE?

When faced with a spiritually or morally difficult situation, we can try to escape it by giving reasons other than the principle truly at issue. For instance, when someone invites you to join in something you know is wrong, how often do you reply, "Doing that is not right, and I don't want to compromise my commitment to Jesus Christ"? Instead, we often say, "Well that sounds nice, but I already have plans." We're not bold to make clear the spiritual issue at stake.

Defile is a strong word that Scripture applies to things the Lord abominates (cf. Lev. 18:24–30). Daniel remained committed to God, even as a prisoner amid a pagan society and even though disobeying the king merited capital punishment. "The fear of man brings a snare" (Prov. 29:25), but an uncompromising character imparts unashamed boldness.

B. Illustrated in the Old Testament

1. Moses demonstrated the boldness of uncompromising character by demanding of Pharaoh, "Let my people go" (Ex. 5:1).

2. The Psalms record insights into David's heart:

   a. Psalm 40:8–10—"I delight to do Your will, O my God; Your Law is within my heart" (v. 8). David says here, "I know Your law, God, and I'm committed to doing it." Any person who has God's law in their heart and desires to obey it can live with the same uncompromising spirit that Daniel and David did. Like Daniel, David also lived out his devotion publicly: "I have proclaimed glad tidings of righteousness in the great congregation; behold, I will not restrain my lips, O Lord, You know. I have not hidden Your righteousness within my heart; I have spoken of Your faithfulness and Your salvation; I have not concealed Your lovingkindness and Your truth from the great congregation" (vv. 9–10). May God make us people like that!

   b. Psalm 71:15—"My mouth shall tell of Your righteousness and of Your salvation all day long." David had godly, unashamed boldness.

3. Daniel 3:13–18, "Nebuchadnezzar in rage and anger gave orders to bring Shadrach, Meshach and Abed-nego; then these men were brought before the king. [He] said to them, 'Is it true, Shadrach, Meshach and Abed-nego, that you do not serve my gods or worship the golden image that I have set up? Now if you are ready, at the

moment you hear the sound of the . . . music, to fall down and worship the image that I have made, very well. But if you do not worship, you will immediately be cast into the midst of a furnace of blazing fire; and what god is there who can deliver you out of my hands?' Shadrach, Meshach and Abed-nego replied to the king, 'O Nebuchadnezzar, we do not need to give you an answer concerning this matter. If it be so, our God whom we serve is able to deliver us from the furnace of blazing fire; and He will deliver us out of your hand, O king. But even if He does not, let it be known to you, O king, that we are not going to serve your gods or worship the golden image that you have set up.'" Daniel's three faithful friends manifested bold and upright character in refusing, no matter what happened, to worship Nebuchadnezzar's image.

C. Illustrated in the New Testament

1. In Jesus' exhortation—"Whoever is ashamed of Me and My words in this adulterous and sinful generation, the Son of Man will also be ashamed of him when He comes in the glory of His Father with the holy angels" (Mark 8:38). What a strong statement.

2. In Peter's encouragement—"If anyone suffers as a Christian, he is not to be ashamed, but is to glorify God in this name" (1 Pet. 4:16). When people ridicule and criticize you for your faith, it's

easy to feel ashamed and afraid to say anything.

3. In Paul's example

   a. Acts 24–26—Near the end of the book of Acts, Paul gave his defense before the rulers Felix, Festus, and Agrippa. Each time, without hesitation, he boldly and unashamedly preached Jesus Christ.

   b. 2 Timothy 1:7–8—Paul exhorted Timothy, "God has not given us a spirit of timidity, but of power and love and discipline. Therefore do not be ashamed of the testimony of our Lord or of me His prisoner."

   c. Philippians 1:20, 27–28—Having expressed his own earnest hope to be bold (v. 20), Paul said, "Only conduct yourselves in a manner worthy of the gospel of Christ, so that whether I come and see you or remain absent, I will hear of you that you are standing firm in one spirit, with one mind striving together for the faith of the gospel; in no way alarmed by your opponents" (vv. 27–28). Paul wanted believers to boldly stand and speak for Christ.

Psalm 119:46 says, "I will also speak of Your testimonies before kings and shall not be ashamed." Uncompromising character has a holy, fearless courage that knows no shame in bearing the name of Jesus Christ—a determination Ezekiel 3:9 calls setting your face like flint, or like a lion (1 Chron. 12:8).

Such boldness is the measure of an uncompromising life. Once you purpose to draw the line wherever God in His Word draws it, you will have, like Daniel, the boldness to speak that Word before kings—undaunted, valiant in truth.

II. AN UNCOMMON STANDARD (DAN. 1:12)

A. Explained

People who pursue an uncompromising life don't live as everyone else does. They inevitably hold an uncommon standard—one that exceeds the norm and surpasses that of the average believer. I remember reading, when I was young, of people exceptionally devoted to praying, and from missionaries' biographies of how differently they lived the Christian life than anybody I knew.

B. Expressed

Daniel expressed that uncommon standard in how he lived. Verse 12 records the diet he requested: "Please . . . let us be given some vegetables to eat and water to drink." Daniel not only respectfully rejected the king's rich food, he demonstrated his commitment to the Lord even through the distinction between his diet and what the rest of the captives ate.

C. Exemplified

Daniel's choice regarding wine is a helpful example.

1. The amorality of wine

   The law did not require abstinence from wine. In fact, the Old Testament indicates that wine was a common part of Jewish society, and when diluted with water, proper to drink.

   a. Exodus 29:40—Wine was Israel's drink offering to God.

   b. 1 Chronicles 9:29—The Temple kept a supply of wine for sacrifices.

   c. Isaiah 24:8–9—Wine was linked to song, gaiety, and revelry.

   d. Isaiah 55:1–2—Wine was a scriptural symbol of salvation's abundance.

2. The abstinence from wine

   Examining who was to abstain from wine helps explain why Daniel chose this standard.

   a. The priest (Lev. 10:8–11)—"The Lord then spoke to Aaron, saying, 'Do not drink wine or strong drink, neither you nor your sons with you, when you come into the tent of meeting, so that you will not die—it is a perpetual statute throughout your generations—and so as to make a distinction between the holy and the profane, and between the unclean and the clean, and so as to teach the sons of Israel all the statutes which the Lord has spoken to them through Moses.'" The Lord set this standard for Aaron, the high priest, and all other serving priests as well, that they might not lose the ability to distinguish between the holy and the unholy, and to rightly lead the people. So total abstinence was required of all functioning priests.

b. The Nazirite (Num. 6:1–4)—"The Lord spoke to Moses, saying, 'Speak to the sons of Israel and say to them, "When a man or woman makes a special vow, the vow of a Nazirite [meaning "to be separated"], to dedicate himself to the Lord, he shall abstain from wine and strong drink; he shall drink no vinegar, whether made from wine or strong drink, nor shall he drink any grape juice nor eat fresh or dried grapes. All the days of his separation he shall not eat anything that is produced by the grape vine, from the seeds even to the skin.""" Not everyone was required to live this way; only those who wanted to live uniquely separated unto God chose such an uncommon standard.

c. The ruler (Prov. 31:4–6)—"It is not for kings, O Lemuel, it is not for kings to drink wine, or for rulers to desire strong drink" (v. 4). Daniel came from a noble family and may have been taught this important principle. Verse 5 explains that rulers should abstain from drinking "lest they drink and forget the law, and pervert the justice of all the afflicted. Give strong drink to him who is perishing, and wine to those who are bitter of heart" (vv. 5–6, NKJV). Wine could be a sedative for a dying man, but it was not meant for those responsible to make important decisions. Great responsibility, especially of a spiritual nature, demands an uncommon standard.

d. The pastor (1 Tim. 5:23)—The apostle Paul told Timothy, "No longer drink water exclusively, but use a little wine for the sake of your stomach and your frequent ailments." It's clear that Timothy didn't customarily drink wine, though that was not specifically commanded of him; he'd chosen an uncommon standard.

e. The prophet (Luke 1:15)—An angel said of John the Baptist, "He will be great in the sight of the Lord; and he will drink no wine or liquor."

f. The elder (Titus 1:7)—One qualification for elders is that they be "not given to wine" (NKJV).

The point is this: Those who desire to live with the most uncompromising commitment establish an uncommon standard. Daniel chose to drink only water and no wine at all, distinguishing himself from the pagan practices of the king's table as well as from gluttony and drunkenness generally. A higher standard doesn't make me more spiritual; it's just one place I can train myself against compromise by holding myself to an uncommon standard—thereby also avoiding all appearance of evil (1 Thess. 5:22). Daniel kept an exceptional standard even against the king's command; how much more easily should we, being free of either command or necessity?

WEAKENED BY WINE

Daniel 5 tells of Belshazzar losing both the Babylonian Empire and his life while in a drunken stupor. Alexander the Great likewise lost his world empire and his life at just thirty-three partly due to drink. Commentator W. A. Criswell notes wine's integral part in the defeat of two French armies: "When the Iron Duke of England, Wellington, was marching his army across the Iberian peninsula, word was brought to his headquarters that ahead of him was a vast store of Spanish wine. He stopped his army. He sent some of his men ahead and they blew it up. Then he marched his army on. It is said that the reason Napoleon Bonaparte lost the battle of Waterloo to the victorious Duke of Wellington was because the night before, Marshall Ney tarried too long over his favorite glass of wine and the next morning his head was clouded and his mind unsteady.

"When France fell in World War II against Hitler, Marshall Petain said, 'France was defeated because its army was drunk.' And the Vichy government of 1940 said the reason for the collapse of the moral fiber of the French army was due to alcohol" (*Expository Sermons on the Book of Daniel* [Grand Rapids: Zondervan, n.d.], 37). Alcohol has undermined many great men and endeavors.

An uncompromising life does not play on the edge of what is right; it chooses that standard which is highest, noblest, and best.

III. AN UNEARTHLY PROTECTION (DAN. 1:9)

In verse 8, "Daniel made up his mind," and in verse 9, "God granted Daniel favor and compassion in the sight of the commander of the officials."

A. The Provision of God's Protection

There are two main possibilities for why Daniel found favor with Ashpenaz:

1. Daniel's integrity

Generally, even if people disagree with your convictions, they admire you for sticking up for them. People don't respect vacillating cowards; they respect individuals with strong moral convictions.

Daniel was gracious, loving, and gentle spirited (vv. 11–13). He had the beautiful character that belongs to the godly. But Scripture doesn't credit Daniel's integrity foremost for shaping Ashpenaz's attitude toward him.

2. God's sovereignty

"Now God granted Daniel favor and compassion" (v. 9). God controls everything. He purposed that Daniel would be His witness in Babylon; it's possibly due to Daniel's influence that the wise men came from the East centuries later, at the birth of Christ. God certainly laid the groundwork through Daniel for the Jews' return to their land after seventy years of captivity. In the same way, God sovereignly moved Ashpenaz to favor Daniel. Nebuchadnezzar in all his power couldn't alter God's plan.

B. The Principles of God's Protection

1. The courage of commitment

Like Daniel, when you live an uncompromising life, you will enjoy supernatural protection. People sometimes ask if I worry what might happen to me for speaking the truth; any natural worry attached to that passes rapidly because I know God has a task for me and will protect me until I complete it.

2. The consequences of commitment

We would do well to trust God, rather than our own compromising, to protect us. Compromise forfeits His unearthly protection and simply leads to further and further compromise, until you are trapped.

C. The Promises of God's Protection

Scripture illustrates how God may bless a man's uncompromising faith by giving him favor with his enemies:

1. 1 Kings 8:50—"Forgive Your people who have sinned against You and all their transgressions which they have transgressed against You, and make them objects of compassion before those who have taken them captive, that they may have compassion on them." Solomon prayed that God would make Israel's then-future captors compassionate, and God did.

2. Psalm 106:45–46—The history of God's people testifies that "He also made them objects of compassion in the presence of all their captors." Why? "He remembered His covenant for their sake and relented according to the greatness of His lovingkindness" (v. 45). As Christians, we too have a covenant with our God in Christ and can be certain of His covenant love.

3. Proverbs 16:7—"When a man's ways are pleasing to the Lord, He makes even his enemies to be at peace with him."

The point of life is to please the Lord. Do that by living with unashamed boldness and holding an uncommon standard, secure in your unearthly protection.

CONCLUSION

The hearts of all men are in the hands of God. The Hebrew for "favor" in Daniel 1:9 speaks to tender love and unfailing compassion, while the word for "compassion" is literally "bowels of compassion"—a gut-level affection. In accomplishing His plan for Daniel, God caused Ashpenaz to love the young captive.

You don't have to play politics to advance God's kingdom. Just don't compromise, and obey God as He places you where He wants. If God wants to lift you up in a society, a church, a ministry, or any other situation, He will work on the hearts of the people you need to reach that place. Don't seek your own advancement; remember God's special care for His faithful people. That care is what lifted Moses from the Nile's reeds to Pharaoh's palace (Ex. 2:3, 5–10). Simply commit to living an uncompromising life and trusting in God's sovereignty.

FOCUSING ON
THE FACTS

1. Connect Daniel's conduct with the principle in Proverbs 29:25. How did David express the same boldness generations earlier in Psalms 40:8–10 and 71:15? Where does that quality show up in the New Testament? What was the foundation for that boldness in all of these instances?

2. Explain the role of an uncommon standard in an uncompromising life.

3. What do you see in common among all of the people and offices which Scripture prohibited from taking alcohol? Explain the principle you see at work there (cf. 1 Thess. 5:22).

4. What was finally responsible for Ashpenaz's favor toward Daniel? How does that principle ultimately underlie the believer's ability to live an uncompromising life?

PONDERING THE PRINCIPLES

1. Read Proverbs 4:23. Why is it important to "watch over your heart with all diligence"? How are you guarding your heart? Try to identify any ways the world's thinking has influenced how you think or live more than God's truth has. How can you be more biblically diligent in those areas? Paul exhorts us to "be alert and sober" since we are "sons of light and sons of day" (1 Thess. 5:5–6). Meditate on whether and how you are cultivating the protection he identifies in verse 8 for shielding our hearts from the world's ways.

2. We'd all love to have unashamed boldness consistently characterize our lives, but it is a quality we must desire and develop in order to acquire. How have you been unashamed for God? How have you been ashamed to be His means of "[opening people's] eyes so that they may turn from darkness to light and from the dominion of Satan to God, that they may receive forgiveness of sins and an inheritance among those who have been sanctified by faith in [Christ]" (Acts 26:18)? Why was Paul unashamed (cf. Rom. 1:16)? Trust God's sovereignty to still be the only power that moves hearts to salvation, and boldly obey the charge in 1 Peter 3:15–16.

3. God was ultimately responsible for sovereignly changing Ashpenaz's heart, but consider how God used Daniel's integrity to accomplish that. If you talked to unbelieving friends or family about how God changes

lives but evidenced to them no such changes in your own life, are you faithfully fulfilling your role in gospel proclamation? Read 1 Peter 1:13–17. Confess to God and repent of anything in your life that would prevent others, even those who know you best, from desiring Him.

THE CONSEQUENCES
OF AN
UNCOMPROMISING
LIFE,
PART 2

INTRODUCTION

It's said that every man has his price. At what point would you abandon your moral standards for personal gain? When does our desire eclipse the standards we say we hold?

There have been people throughout history who would not compromise, no matter the price. Martin Luther at the Diet of Worms refused to recant his faithfulness to Christ, even on threat of death. Hugh Latimer and Nicholas Ridley, two English reformers, were both burned at the stake for their faith in Christ. Such people have no price— they cannot be bought.

On the other hand, we commonly hear of people who boast their moral standards and extol their own righteous character, yet sell out when compromise appears more beneficial. And it's not always obvious to a person when he's compromising.

A. Examples of Compromise Today

People say they believe the Bible—but stay in churches where the Bible isn't taught. People claim convictions about sin—until that sin is committed by their own children. People say they oppose dishonesty and corruption—until that means confronting their boss and likely losing their job. People have high moral standards—until their lusts are kindled by an unholy relationship and they rationalize their compromise. People are honest—until just a little dishonesty will save them a lot of money. People know something is definitely wrong—but will cover up the truth for the sake of keeping the peace. People claim a conviction—but will directly violate it for someone whose favor they seek. People know what ought to be said—but don't say it for fear of losing face.

B. Examples of Compromise in the Bible

Adam compromised God's law, followed his wife's sin, and lost paradise (Gen. 3:6, 22–24). Abraham compromised the truth, lied about Sarah, and nearly lost his wife (Gen. 12:10–20). Sarah compromised God's Word by sending Abraham to Hagar, who bore Ishmael, and lost peace in the Middle East (Gen. 16:1–4, 11–12). Esau compromised for a meal and lost his birthright (Gen. 25:29–34). Saul compromised his obedience to God's divine command and lost his kingdom (1 Sam. 15:3, 20–28). Aaron compromised his and the people's obedience, and they all lost the privilege of entering the Promised Land (Num. 20:24; cf. Ps. 95:8–11). Samson compromised his devotion as a Nazirite with Delilah and lost his strength, his eyes, and his life (Judg. 16:4–6, 16–30). Israel compromised the commands of the Lord, lived in sin, and lost the ark of God to the Philistines (1 Sam. 4:1–11). David compromised the standards of God, committed adultery with Bathsheba, murdered Uriah, and lost his infant son (2 Sam. 11:1–12:23). Solomon compromised by marrying foreign wives and lost the kingdom (1 Kings 11:1–8). Ahab compromised, married Jezebel, and lost his throne (1 Kings 16:30–33; 21:1–19; 22:34–38). Israel compromised the law of God with sin and idolatry and lost their homeland (2 Chron. 36:14–17).

Peter compromised his allegiance to Christ and lost his joy (Mark 14:66–72). Later, he also compromised the truth of the church's unity for acceptance with the Judaizers, and he lost his liberty (Gal. 2:11–14). Ananias and Sapphira compromised their truthfulness, lied to the Holy Spirit, and lost their lives (Acts 5:1–11). Judas compromised his connection to Christ for thirty pieces of silver and lost his eternal soul (Matt. 26:20–25, 47–49, 27:1–5; cf. John 17:12).

C. Examples of Commitment

In contrast, Scripture shows us those who wouldn't compromise, no matter the price—Moses before Pharaoh; David at multiple points in his life; Paul before Festus, Felix, and Agrippa. But there's no better biblical illustration of an undefiled, uncompromising man than Daniel. During his long life in Babylon amid the pagan Chaldeans, he never compromised his convictions.

THE "CADET PRAYER"

West Point cadets recite a prayer in each chapel service, which includes the words, "Make us to choose the harder right instead of the easier wrong, and never to be content with a half truth when the whole can be won. Endow us with courage that is born of loyalty to all that is noble and worthy, that scorns to compromise with vice and injustice and knows no fear when truth and right are in jeopardy."

R E V I E W

We have examined three characteristics of an uncompromising life:

I. AN UNASHAMED BOLDNESS (DAN. 1:8)

II. AN UNCOMMON STANDARD (DAN. 1:12)

III. AN UNEARTHLY PROTECTION (DAN. 1:9)

A. The Provision of God's Protection

B. The Principles of God's Protection

C. The Promises of God's Protection

L E S S O N

D. The Parallels of God's Protection

Joseph and Daniel shared many parallels. Both young men were taken captive to foreign kingdoms, where they eventually served as prime minister. Both possessed extraordinary prophetic powers, which God used to elevate them to prominence. And both, with God's protection, were able to confound the pretenders and phonies that surrounded them.

God often elevates the person who lives

uncompromisingly. It's been said that politics is the art of compromise, and it's true that most people in high places have reached those places by compromising somewhere along the line. But know that God will put you in whatever position He desires, without requiring your compromise.

IV. AN UNHINDERED PERSISTENCE (DAN. 1:10–11)

A. Ashpenaz's Dilemma (v. 10)

"And the commander of the officials said to Daniel, 'I am afraid of my lord the king, who has appointed your food and your drink; for why should he see your faces looking more haggard than the youths who are your own age? Then you would make me forfeit my head to the king.'"

Interestingly, Ashpenaz gives Daniel the reason for his hesitation; that shows that he did view the young captives compassionately. Still, he would not risk capital punishment should they appear worse than their peers under his care.

B. Daniel's Determination (v. 11)

1. Recorded in Daniel

Without growing disrespectful, Daniel persists with his request. "Then Daniel said to the overseer" (v. 11)—this steward, under Ashpenaz, "the commander of the officials," was "appointed over Daniel, Hananiah, Mishael and Azariah."

So interestingly, when he was unable to get a desired answer from Ashpenaz, Daniel appealed, undaunted, to a lower court, as it were—to a man who didn't bear the burden of direct accountability to the king.

An uncompromising spirit never gives up. It's common to hear excuses like, "I knew what I should do, and I tried to do it, but it just didn't work out," or, "I had no choice; the others were all doing that." But an uncompromising character will never abandon principle, even when the first door seems closed.

2. Repeated by Paul

On his way to Jerusalem, Paul was met by the prophet Agabus, who "bound his own feet and hands" with Paul's belt in illustration of what awaited the apostle in the city (Acts 21:10–11). But Paul already knew his fate: "The Holy Spirit solemnly testifies to me in every city, saying that bonds and afflictions await me. But I do not consider my life of any account as dear to myself, so that I may finish my course and the ministry which I received from the Lord Jesus, to testify solemnly of the gospel of the grace of God" (20:23–24). When an opportunity closed in one place, Paul simply went to another (16:6–10); he was never looking for an out. An uncompromising life persists.

V. AN UNBLEMISHED FAITH (DAN. 1:12–13)

A. The Principle Explained

Daniel believed that God would make a way for him to obey. Sin fosters doubt; holiness yields confidence in God and what He is accomplishing

1. Romans 8:31—"If God is for us, who can be against us?" (NKJV)

2. Isaiah 43:2, 5—The Lord promised His chosen people Israel, "When you pass through the waters, I will be with you; and through the rivers, they will not overflow you. When you walk through the fire, you will not be scorched, nor will the flame burn you. Do not fear, for I am with you."

When you're trusting in the Lord, as shown by your pure heart and pure life, you'll be able to live with the same kind of invincible faith Daniel and Paul had.

B. The Principle Enacted

"Please test your servants for ten days, and let us be given some vegetables to eat and water to drink. Then let our appearance be observed in your presence and the appearance of the youths who are eating the king's choice food; and deal with your servants according to what you see" (vv. 12–13).

Daniel was risking his neck. But his faith in the Lord—despite having lived through terrible national disaster and God's seeming abandonment of Judah—gave Daniel the confidence of a pure heart and an uncompromising spirit.

His request for vegetables only wasn't due to any inherent virtue to a vegetarian diet; it was the food of the poor. Realistically, ten days of vegetables versus ten days of the king's food wouldn't produce any big physiological difference. Daniel was counting on the Lord to honor His Word; perhaps the young man proposed this test based on the Lord's revelation, given Daniel's confidence and the Lord's answer in it.

God honors the life that pursues obedience to His Word no matter the temporal consequences. That's an unblemished faith. Do you believe that the way to true joy and happiness is to stand against sin and evil, no matter the circumstances? If you do, then you won't compromise.

VI. AN UNUSUAL TEST (DAN. 1:14–16)

A. The Steward's Evaluation (v. 14)

"So he listened to them in this matter and tested them for ten days."

All commitment is tested. James 1:2–3 speaks of the trials that test our faith to prove its genuineness. When Daniel literally staked his life on God's Word, the test of his faith immediately followed.

B. God's Intervention (vv. 15–16)

1. Passing the test (v. 15)

> "At the end of ten days their appearance seemed better and they were fatter than all the youths who had been eating the king's choice food."

> They looked healthier and more vigorous than the others; God obviously caused this outcome.

2. Avoiding the defilement (v. 16)

> "So the overseer continued to withhold their choice food and the wine they were to drink, and kept giving them vegetables."

> God honored Daniel and his three friends' determination to avoid the ungodly lifestyle the Chaldeans wanted to impose on them.

God richly blessed their faithfulness not to compromise His Word with the world. This passage brings together the wonderful dual truths of God's sovereignty and man's responsibility. The success of "these four youths" (v. 17) depended on their own commitment; but everything was entirely in God's control. Both are true.

VII. AN UNMEASURABLE BLESSING (DAN. 1:17–20)

A. The Benefits of God's Blessing (v. 17)

1. To all the youths

> "As for these four youths, God gave them

knowledge and intelligence in every branch of literature and wisdom . . ."

God gave them all they needed for productive, godly living in Babylon's society of advanced learning—not only the ability to understand that culture and its technologies, but also the wisdom to apply His Word to their situation.

2. To Daniel

". . . Daniel even understood all kinds of visions and dreams."

God uniquely enabled Daniel to interpret dreams and visions, both of which were means of divine revelation at the time. Thus, God established Daniel as a seer or prophet, one who receives God's Word, which sets up the rest of Daniel's prophecy in this book.

B. The Results of God's Blessing (vv. 18–20)

1. Their success (vv. 18–19)

"Then at the end of the days [the three years of training] which the king had specified for presenting them, the commander of the officials presented them before Nebuchadnezzar. The king talked with them, and out of them all not one was found like Daniel, Hananiah, Mishael and Azariah . . ."

The king personally examined all of the young

men who had been deported in 606 BC—recall that the second and third groups of captives would not come until 597 and 586, respectively—upon the completion of their training. And Daniel, Hananiah, Mishael, and Azariah graduated *summa cum laude*—at the top of the class. You do not have to compromise to achieve a degree of excellence that even the world cannot deny.

2. Their service (v. 19)

". . . so they entered the king's personal service."

Literally, this phrase is "stood before the king." Recall that that means they served him, and incorporates the idea of waiting to take and deliver the king's message or command. Imagine standing alongside a foreign nation's conqueror king, in his royal court, having been lifted by God to that place at the age of seventeen or eighteen. And Scripture never tells of Daniel compromising in all the seventy years he ruled in Babylon as prime minister (Dan. 2:48; cf. 6:1–2).

3. Their superiority (v. 20)

"As for every matter of wisdom and understanding about which the king consulted them, he found them ten times better than all the magicians and conjurers who were in all his realm."

As Christians, we have the revelation of God and the indwelling Spirit, so we are far wiser than the most intelligent unbeliever. So remain true to the Word of God, stand up boldly for what you believe, and let nothing intimidate you into compromising what you know to be the absolute, inviolable truth. Hold your convictions with the same love and graciousness Daniel showed, and trust God to place you, full of honor and blessing, where He will.

VIII. AN UNLIMITED INFLUENCE (DAN. 1:21)

"And Daniel continued until the first year of Cyrus the king."

Daniel's integrity and longevity in his appointed position had far-reaching results. I see his influence in Cyrus's decree sending Israel back from exile in Ezra 1, in the Jews' rebuilding Jerusalem's wall under Nehemiah, and eventually in the Eastern wise men coming to crown the King who was born in Bethlehem. Daniel undergirds the history of the Messiah and the Messiah's people. His influence continues, unlimited, through his prophecy of the history of the world until the reign of Messiah, who is "King of kings, and Lord of lords" (Rev. 19:16) who reigns forever.

CONCLUSION

Beloved, do not compromise. Submit yourself to the Lord,

to do with as He pleases, that you may know the blessing of His greatness.

FOCUSING ON THE FACTS

1. Why didn't Ashpenaz honor Daniel's request? With what attitude did Daniel persist in his request? How was he able to maintain that attitude?

2. Physical benefits aside, what was the primary benefit in God protecting Daniel and his friends from partaking of the king's food and wine? How does this demonstrate God's covenant faithfulness?

3. What additional privilege did Daniel receive (v. 17)? How did God's giftings uniquely equip each of these young men for the service He intended for them, and bless subsequent generations (vv. 18–21)?

PONDERING THE PRINCIPLES

1. Think of a time when you had to persist—or maybe should have persisted—in making a request, as Daniel did. Why did or didn't you pursue your request? Were you able to do so with unblemished faith like Daniel's? How was that faith tested? What was the basis of Daniel's faith? How does your own compare?

2. Consider what sin did to King David's confidence before God. Not only does sin bring doubt, it yields a fear of divine discipline and a loss of joy as well (Ps. 51:1–12). Living in obedience gives you the courage of conviction and the fruit of confidence because you are in line with the Lord's will and work. If you are trusting in Christ's sufficient work for your salvation but still feel no courage or confidence, perhaps you are harboring some impurity in your life. Examine yourself carefully before the Lord, and make verses 7–10 your prayer to Him.

UNCOMPROMISING FAITH

IN THE FIERY FURNACE,

PART 1

INTRODUCTION

A. Worshiping the Wrong God

The core issue in Daniel 3 hits a constant theme of Scripture, and indeed of human history: It is the conflict between those who honor God in His rightful place and those who refuse to.

1. Scripture on idolatry

Man is incurably religious. All peoples and ethnic groups have some form of worship—of either the true God or some false substitute, but man is by nature a worshiper.

a. Explained

Romans 1:21 says, "Even though [men] knew God, they did not honor Him as God," instead worshiping "the creature rather than the Creator" (v. 25). Turning away from God, mankind began to worship man, birds, beasts, and other creatures (v. 23). Romans 1 is clear that a person who rejects God doesn't enter a religious vacuum; he will still worship someone or something.

The Old Testament reveals that man characteristically creates a god like himself and then becomes like that god. Doing so accommodates his sinfulness, since one difficulty in worshiping the true God is having to face our own inadequacy and sinfulness. A god who is like us is much easier to live with than a holy God.

Psalm 115 gives insight into that process. Verses 1–8 say, "Not to us, O Lord, not to us, but to Your name give glory because of Your lovingkindness, because of Your truth. Why should the nations say, 'Where, now, is their God?' But our God is in the heavens; He does whatever He pleases. Their idols are silver and gold, the work of man's hands. They have mouths, but they cannot speak; they have eyes, but they cannot see; they have ears, but they cannot hear; they have noses, but they cannot smell; they have hands, but they cannot feel; they have feet, but they cannot walk; they cannot make a sound with their throat. Those who make them will become like them, everyone who trusts in them." The Bible says that "God created man in His own image" (Gen. 1:27). But man creates gods in his image—the ultimate rebellion. So continual conflict exists between the worship of the true God and the worship of gods fashioned by the imagination of men.

b. Illustrated

The Old Testament repeatedly mentions a god called Baal, a title which simply means "lord." The Canaanites believed that Baal was the force behind human sexuality; therefore, any sexual act was an expression of Baal's power and was sacred. The temples of Baal housed priestesses who were known as sacred prostitutes and considered holy women; to have intercourse with them was believed to unite one with Baal and his power.

Man invents gods that accommodate his vile sinfulness. And inevitably, those gods lead people into immorality because they reflect the sinfulness of their inventors.

c. Denounced

1) Romans 1

Men knew God but did not glorify Him as God, and exchanged His glory for a mere image, an idol (Rom. 1:21, 23). "Therefore God gave them over in the lusts of their hearts to impurity, so that their bodies would be dishonored among them" (v. 24). The rejection of the true God in verse 21 swiftly leads to the establishment of false gods in verses 22–23, and the consequent immorality of verses 24–32—so thoroughgoing that it gives "hearty approval to those who practice [the same]" (v. 32).

2) Exodus 20

Idolatry is one of God's foundational concerns regarding man. It leads off the Ten Commandments, the Lord saying, "You shall have no other gods before Me. You shall not make for yourself an idol, or any likeness of what is in heaven above or on the earth beneath or in the water under the earth. You shall not worship them or serve them; for I, the Lord your God, am a jealous God, visiting the iniquity of the fathers on the children, on the third and the fourth generations of those who hate Me, but showing lovingkindness to thousands, to those who love Me and keep My commandments" (Ex. 20:3–6).

The Bible is explicit that there is no god but the true God (Deut. 6:4; Isa. 43:11; 44:6; 45:5–6). And it denounces all idols, whether of stone, wood, or metal, or of the mind or emotions; tangible or intangible, external or internal, all idols are forbidden in the charge: "You shall have no other gods before Me. You shall not make for yourself an idol."

d. Examined

A brief survey of Scripture's teaching on idolatry helps reveal what Hananiah, Azariah, and Mishael (Shadrach, Meshach, and Abednego) faced in Daniel 3. Even though they didn't have God's full revelation as we do in the complete Bible today, they had enough to know that they could not please Him by bowing to the image of gold.

1) Idolatry illustrated

a) Bowing to images (Ex. 20:5)

b) Worshiping images or other gods (Deut. 30:17; Ps. 106:19–20; Isa. 44:17), angels (Col. 2:18), the host of heaven (Deut. 4:19), devils (Matt. 4:9–10), or dead men (Ps. 106:28)

c) Sacrificing to images or other gods (Ex. 22:20; Ps. 106:38)

d) Swearing by (Josh. 23:7), walking after (Deut. 8:19), speaking in the name of (Deut. 18:20), looking to (Hos. 3:1), serving (Jer. 5:19), or fearing other gods (2 Kings 17:35)

e) Setting up idols in the heart (Ezek. 14:3–4)

f) Coveting (Eph. 5:5)

g) Sensuality (Phil. 3:19)

2) Idolatry condemned

a) Abominable to God (Deut. 7:25)

b) Hateful to God (Deut. 16:22)

c) Vain and foolish (Ps. 115:4–8)

d) Profane (Ezek. 23:39)

e) Anarchic (1 Pet. 4:3)

f) Useless (Judg. 10:14)

g) Devoid of sense (Rom. 1:21–23)

h) Defiling (Ezek. 20:7)

3) Idolatry's consequences

a) Forgetting God and entering futility (Jer. 18:15)

b) Straying into punishment (Ezek. 44:10)

    c) Profaning the name of God (Ezek. 20:39)

    d) Defiling what is holy (Ezek. 5:11)

    e) Estrangement from God (Ezek. 14:5)

    f) Forsaking God and provoking His wrath (2 Kings 22:17)

    g) Hating God and bringing wrath on yourself (2 Chron. 19:2)

    h) Ingratitude and spurning God (Deut. 31:20)

4) Idolatry's judgment

    a) For Israel

        i) Judicial death (Deut. 17:2–5)

        ii) Dreadful judgment that ends in death (Jer. 8:2)

        iii) Banishment (Amos 5:26–27)

    b) For all

        i) Exclusion from heaven (1 Cor. 6:9–10)

        ii) Eternal torment (Rev. 21:8)

Idolatry is a grave offense to God. The Bible's warnings about it boil down to having nothing to do with idols: to flee from them (1 Cor. 10:14), have no "fellowship with demons" (v. 20, NKJV), and "guard yourselves from idols" (1 John 5:21).

2. Idolatry in society

Some argue that our sophisticated society today, with its Judeo-Christian foundations, could harbor no idols. But recall that while idolatry is external in many societies, in others it is primarily internal. Millions in our world who would never think of bowing to a stone idol spend their lives worshiping some useless god established in their own minds.

An idol is anything you value before God. Some common idols of the modern day include:

a. Possessions

Possessions can usurp the place of God in your life. Do you spend more time thinking about possessions than God? Do you spend more energy on acquiring them or preserving your standard of living than on knowing God? If so, that is a good indication that you have a problem in this area.

b. Plenty

Colossians 3:5 says that covetousness is idolatry. To covet something is to worship it, like the rich man who decided to build bigger barns to store his crops in (Luke 12:16–21). He planned to have so much that he could relax and eat, drink, and be merry, but the Lord replied, "You fool! This very night your soul is required of you" (v. 20).

c. Pride

Our society's primary god is the love of self. In fact, some in our society unashamedly see themselves as gods.

d. People

Others idolize another person—a child, a mate, a lover, a friend. In contrast, Hannah long prayed for a son, and when God gave her Samuel, she didn't worship the child. Rather, she committed him to the Lord's service (1 Sam. 1:9–28). Abraham, also, waited for a son until he was one hundred years old, but when God tested Abraham's faith by directing him to sacrifice Isaac, Abraham demonstrated that his love for and trust in God exceeded even his love for his son (Gen. 22:1–14).

Of course that doesn't mean you shouldn't love or be committed to other people. You simply must keep your priorities in the right order.

SINGLE-MINDED SERVICE

The great nineteenth-century English preacher Charles

H. Spurgeon on one occasion arrived with his fiancée where he was going to preach. They were separated in the jostling crowd of thousands pushing in to hear him. When he failed to find her after the meeting, he went to her house, where he found her pouting. Mrs. Spurgeon herself wrote, "Quietly he let me tell him how indignant I had felt . . . . [He assured] me of his deep affection for me, but [pointed] out that, before all things, he was *God's servant*, and I must be prepared to yield my claims to His.

"I never forgot the teaching of that day; I had learned my hard lesson by heart, for I do not recollect ever again seeking to assert my right to his time and attention when any service for God demanded them" (*C. H. Spurgeon Autobiography*, vol. 1 [Carlisle, Penn.: Banner of Truth, 1962], 288–89).

---

e. Pleasure

Our society also worships the god of entertainment. Amusement parks are full of people trying to escape the reality of life by enjoying a fantasy world. Lots of people pay a lot of money for just a few moments of excitement. Our society is full of thrill-seekers, the sensual—lovers of pleasure rather than lovers of God (2 Tim. 3:1–5).

f. Projects

Some people immerse themselves in projects and organizations, such as the Parent-Teacher Association, Little League, world peace, politics, hobbies, religious programs, or the Rotary Club. Seeking for meaning, they fill their lives with projects.

g. Prominence

Others live for recognition. They want the best places at fashionable or influential tables, and love to see their names in print.

All such idols end up on the trash heap of an empty, burned-out life. But people will always find something to worship. And how stubbornly we cling to our idols!

B. Worshiping the Right God in the Wrong Way

1. Explained

Scripture is clear that it's not only wrong to worship something other than God; it's wrong to worship the true God in a wrong way.

When Aaron and the Israelites made the golden calf in Exodus 32, they intended it to represent the true God, but it was still an instance of unacceptable worship.

God told Saul to utterly destroy the Amalekites and all that was theirs (1 Sam. 15:1–3), but Saul spared their king and the best animals and goods (vv. 4–9). When Samuel confronted Saul about his disobedience, Saul claimed to have taken the animals to sacrifice to God (vv. 10–25). Samuel replied, "You have rejected the word of the Lord, and the Lord has rejected you from being king over Israel" (vv. 26–29). We honor God by worshiping Him as He commands, not however we choose.

2. Illustrated

a. In the church's history

The medieval church faced the iconoclastic (from Gk., *eikōn*, "image") controversy over the excessive use of statues and images in worship. Even today, the inclusion of crucifixes and other images in worship constitute a kind of idolatry. The common claim is that worshipers don't actually worship the icons, which simply serve as representations. But the transition from worshiping the God behind the statue to worshiping the statue itself is subtle.

b. In Israel's history

1) The provision of salvation

Recall when the Lord sent fiery serpents among the Israelites for their rebellion against Him and Moses. Many were bitten and died. Numbers 21:7–8 says, "So the people came to Moses and said, 'We have sinned, because we have spoken against the Lord and you; intercede with the Lord, that He may remove the serpents from us.' And Moses interceded for the people. Then the Lord said to Moses, 'Make a fiery serpent, and set it on a standard; and it shall come about, that everyone who is bitten, when he looks at it, he will live.'" The serpent on the pole was merely a symbol of God's power, but looking at the pole was how the people demonstrated their faith.

2) The perversion of the serpent

Later in Israel's history, King Hezekiah of Judah ushered in a great revival. As part of that, 2 Kings 18:4 says, "He removed the high places and broke down the sacred pillars and cut down the Asherah. He also broke in pieces the bronze serpent that Moses had made, for until those days the sons of Israel burned incense to it; and it was called Nehushtan" ("the little brass thing"). What began as a symbol became an idol. That is always the danger with an icon because man is an idolater.

Scripture forbids all idolatry—both worship of a false god and worship of the true God in a false way. And Daniel's three friends knew this well.

LESSON

I. THE CEREMONY (DAN. 3:1–3)

A. The Act of Idolatry (v. 1)

"Nebuchadnezzar the king made an image of gold, the height of which was sixty cubits and its width six cubits; he set it up on the plain of Dura in the province of Babylon."

Nebuchadnezzar was indisputably the greatest monarch of his day. But his idolatrous act of establishing this enormous image clashes with his confession to Daniel in the previous chapter. After God enabled Daniel to interpret the dream that had confounded Nebuchadnezzar and all his advisors, the king "fell on his face and did homage to Daniel . . . and said, 'Surely your God is a God of gods and a Lord of kings and a revealer of mysteries, since you have been able to reveal this mystery'" (2:46–47). But even that clear demonstration of God's power didn't subdue the Babylonian king's ego; two verses later, Nebuchadnezzar builds an idol to himself. In fact, Daniel's interpretation of his dream, which depicted Nebuchadnezzar as the golden head over all the earth, superior to successive world powers (vv. 36–38), may have spurred on the king's massive ego.

1. The image

   a. Its dimensions

   ". . . the height of which was sixty cubits and its width six cubits . . ."

   A cubit was measured from the elbow to the end of the hand, approximately eighteen inches, so sixty cubits equals about ninety feet. At only six cubits (nine feet) wide, this was an extremely tall, thin statue. It was probably a huge human form, but its ten-to-one proportions depart significantly from the five-to-one proportions of most human beings; it is possible that some of that height came from a towering pedestal.

   b. Its construction

   ". . . an image of gold . . ."

   For the image to be solid gold would have been prohibitive in cost as well as construction and transportation. It was common in ancient times to overlay figures of wood with gold (cf. Isa. 40:19; 41:7). But the cost and difficulty of even that, for a figure of such dimensions, would have been immense.

THE SIGNIFICANCE OF A SYSTEM OF SIXES

While our decimal system is based on tens, the Babylonians based their system on sixes. Daniel's use of that sexagesimal system in giving the dimensions for the image of gold refutes higher critics' claim that the book does not date from the Babylonian era. Liberal scholars date the writing of Daniel close to the time of Christ in order to explain away its prophetic portions as after-the-fact accounts rather than divine prophecy. The text itself, however, doesn't warrant that.

---

c. Its location

"... he set it up on the plain of Dura in the province of Babylon."

The plain of Dura was quite flat. Surely such a statue would have been visible for a great distance. Imagine how that region's bright sun would have sparkled off the gold in an incredible display of grandeur.

2. The intentions

Nebuchadnezzar was an intelligent man—one

of the world's greatest architects, statesmen, and military strategists. What did he intend this huge image to accomplish?

a. Unifying the nation

A leader unifies his nation around a common objective. The Caesars later also used emperor worship to unify the Roman Empire.

b. Verifying loyalty

Nebuchadnezzar wanted all of his officials to demonstrate their loyalty and faithfulness to him by bowing—it was a test.

c. Preventing factions

He also wanted a single religion so that no other allegiances could compete in the hearts of his subjects and potentially fracture the empire.

d. Glorifying self

Finally, this system served Nebuchadnezzar's unmatched ego—he desired that all might worship him. Centuries later, Herod displayed the same attitude in Acts 12. He delivered a speech to the people, who cried, "The voice of a god, and not of a man!" (v. 22). Verse 23 records the result of such pride: "Immediately an angel of the Lord struck him because he did not give God the glory, and he was eaten by worms and died."

Recall the perennial conflict chapter 3 shows us, between worshiping the true God and worshiping a false god in the form of this self-centered, humanistic king. It's a choice everyone continually makes—even Christians.

B. The Acceptance of the Invitation (vv. 2–3)

1. The recipients (v. 2)

"Then Nebuchadnezzar the king sent word to assemble . . ."

a. "the satraps"—the top governors of the provinces in the Babylonian Empire

b. "the prefects and the governors"—likely rulers of smaller subdivisions of the provinces

c. "the counselors"—the lawyers who made up the cabinets and senates

d. "the treasurers"—the masters of government funds

e. "the judges"—the chief arbitrators or provincial counselors throughout the empire

f. "the magistrates"—the officers who carried out judicial sentences and administered the law locally

g. "and all the rulers of the provinces"— Daniel 3:2 concludes with Nebuchadnezzar having invited everybody who was anybody "to come to the dedication of the image that Nebuchadnezzar the king had set up." Nebuchadnezzar wanted absolutely everybody's allegiance.

2. The subtle repetition (v. 3)

"Then the satraps, the prefects and the governors, the counselors, the treasurers, the judges, the magistrates and all the rulers of the provinces were assembled for the dedication of the image that Nebuchadnezzar the king had set up; and they stood before the image that Nebuchadnezzar had set up."

Why the repetition? Translators of the Septuagint, the Greek-language version of the Old Testament, left out verse 3 because they believed it unnecessary. But the repetition in verse 3 of all of these officials is an almost humorous insight into the lack of personal integrity among the leaders of the empire—none of them had the courage to deny Nebuchadnezzar his megalomania. Only three men in the entire Babylonian empire had that kind of integrity.

FOCUSING ON
THE FACTS

1. What do all people have in common regarding worship?
   If people refuse to worship the true God, what will they
   worship? Explain the cycle of idolatry; why does man
   create a god like himself?

2. Explain from Scripture why idolatry constitutes man's
   ultimate form of rebellion.

3. Besides worshiping wrong gods, what is another form
   of idolatry? Explain how Exodus 32 and 1 Samuel 15
   illustrate that truth.

4. Why did the medieval church dispute so seriously over the use of icons? How did Israel demonstrate the sin tendency that the medieval church sought to guard against (cf. Num. 21:6–9; 2 Kings 18:4)?

5. What did Nebuchadnezzar seek to accomplish by erecting the image?

6. Explain the significance of the repetition of the list of Babylonian rulers in Daniel 3:2–3.

PONDERING THE PRINCIPLES

1. What do you idolize? If you can't answer that, think of what you love, in practice, more than you love God—what do you spend your time and other resources on? Do those things distract you from prayer and the Word? Do you struggle to give them up? Repent of those idols, and consider from Scripture what you can do today to rearrange your priorities—from your heart outward. What attitudes and practices should you put off and put on? Choose practical goals and means to motivate yourself to maintain your biblical commitments. Finally, find someone to hold you accountable before the Lord.

2. Do you know why you believe what you believe? Do you stand up for the truth even under pressure? Imagine yourself with a group of non-Christians at work or in your neighborhood. If they ridiculed you for loving Christ, how would you defend the faith (Jude 1:3)? Read 1 Peter 3:14–15, and write out a few sentences that could serve as a gracious, effective answer in situations ranging from honest questions to intimidation and ridicule.

UNCOMPROMISING FAITH

IN THE FIERY FURNACE,

PART 2

INTRODUCTION

Our attitudes, decisions, and behavior are determined by one of two things: external pressure or internal principles. The conflict between those two elements is constant. And given our skill at self-justification, we easily succumb to external pressures that we try to redefine as internal principles. The fundamental question is this: Do we live by biblical principles and convictions or by the pressures of our particular situation?

We're all weary of insincere people acting for social or political expedience. If ever the world needed principled people, it needs them now.

As followers of Jesus Christ, we have a lot to learn from the three young men in Daniel chapter 3. I want you to put yourself in the context of this passage and honestly evaluate how you would respond in a similar situation. Would you put God and His Word first?

REVIEW

I. THE CEREMONY (DAN. 3:1–3)

LESSON

II. THE COMMAND (DAN. 3:4–7)

A. The Call of the Herald (v. 4)

"Then the herald loudly proclaimed: 'To you the command is given, O peoples, nations and men of every language . . .'"

"Peoples, nations and men of every language" simply indicates a broad conglomerate of people; it was also used in verses 7 and 29, as well as in 4:1 and 6:25. This command applied widely.

B. The Cue by the Orchestra (v. 5)

". . . that at the moment you hear the sound of the horn, flute, lyre, trigon, psaltery, bagpipe and all kinds of music, you are to fall down and worship the golden image that Nebuchadnezzar the king has set up."

Nebuchadnezzar demanded absolute submission with exacting precision. He instructed his royal orchestra to give the cue. It would have sounded very different to anything we're accustomed to—quite dissonant and primarily designed to draw everyone's attention to the image they were to bow to.

The "horn" had a relatively low sound; the "flute" produced a higher tone. The "lyre" was a small, high-sounding harp; the "trigon" is best understood to refer to an ancient, triangular harp. The "psaltery" was a harp with a sounding board that produced a lower sound than a lyre. And the "bagpipe." At the time all these instruments sounded, everyone was instantly to fall down and worship the image.

C. The Consequences of Disobedience (v. 6)

"But whoever does not fall down and worship shall immediately be cast into the midst of a furnace of blazing fire."

The word "blazing" simply intensifies the threat—refusing to bow down constituted a treasonous act. Standing in opposition to the king's authority meant death.

D. The Conformity of the People (v. 7)

"Therefore at that time, when all the peoples heard the sound of the horn, flute, lyre, trigon, psaltery, bagpipe and all kinds of music, all the peoples, nations and men of every language fell down and worshiped the golden image that Nebuchadnezzar the king had set up."

We meet in this verse a group of intimidated people who typify the approach to life of doing whatever is expedient, whatever they need to do to get by. They willingly compromised in order to keep whatever they had.

But not everyone caved.

III. THE CONSPIRACY (DAN. 3:8–12)

A. The Context of the Accusation (v. 8)

"For this reason at that time certain Chaldeans came forward and brought charges against the Jews."

As many as seventy-five Judean young men were taken captive to Babylon, but of them all, Scripture records only four—Daniel and his three friends—as having been uncompromising. And notice that Shadrach, Meshach, and Abed-nego didn't simply ride Daniel's coattails in character—although Daniel apparently was absent for this episode, his friends demonstrated tremendous conviction for young men only about twenty years old.

"Chaldeans" made the accusation, likely from resentment over Daniel and his friends' promotion in the empire. Daniel 2:49 records, "Daniel made request of the king, and he appointed Shadrach, Meshach and Abed-nego over the administration of the province of Babylon, while Daniel was at the king's court." Daniel was promoted to prime minister of Babylon, and the other three were placed in leadership over the province of Babylon.

"Brought charges against" sounds like legal terminology, but a literal translation of that phrase is "ate the pieces of." The imagery is of a rapacious animal stripping flesh and tissue off its prey to consume it. The Chaldeans came to the king as if they were defending him, appearing to aid him in enforcing his command. But they aggressively desired to destroy these Jews, as if by dismemberment and devouring, from hatred and malice. And we know they were energized by Satan and his evil religious system in that nation to want to tear into these young Hebrews.

B. The Cause for the Accusation (vv. 9–12*a*)

"They responded and said to Nebuchadnezzar the king: 'O king, live forever! You, O king, have made a decree that every man who hears the sound of the horn, flute, lyre, trigon, psaltery, and bagpipe and all kinds of music, is to fall down and worship the golden image. But whoever does not fall down and worship shall be cast into the midst of a furnace of blazing fire. There are certain Jews whom you have appointed over the administration of the province of Babylon, namely Shadrach, Meshach and Abed-nego.'"

The Chaldeans flattered the king and accurately reiterated his standard before revealing what truly bothered them: that these "certain Jews" should be given high-ranking positions. They despised having imported hostages, subjugated foreigners, rule over them. Proverbs 14:30 says, "A sound heart is life to the body, but envy is rottenness to the bones" (NKJV); Song of Solomon 8:6 speaks of "jealousy as cruel as the grave" (NKJV)—corrosive and consuming.

C. The Content of the Accusation (v. 12*b*)

1. Their lack of regard

   "These men, O king, have disregarded you . . ."

   The first part of the Chaldeans' threefold accusation was that Shadrach, Meshach, and Abed-nego refused to show proper respect due the king. But that was not true, as chapter 1 showed. They were good citizens. They had responded to the king appropriately by attending his ceremony. They had demonstrated the submission later taught by our Lord in Matthew 22:21: "Render to Caesar the things that are Caesar's; and to God the things that are God's." They had unquestionably fulfilled their responsibility to the king as far as they could without violating their greater responsibility to God.

2. Their religious limitation

". . . they do not serve your gods or worship the golden image which you have set up."

The rest of the Chaldeans' accusation was true, however. These three young men knew the price of disobedience and were willing to pay it. They lived by their internal, biblical principles and demonstrated great character by withstanding the external pressure of the entire mass of people bowing down.

Consider the situation: Nebuchadnezzar had been good to them, and he held their destiny in his hands. Resisting him was useless and utterly undermined their futures. They could have reasoned, *An idol is nothing anyway, so why not just kneel down with everyone else but pray to the true God? If we don't, we'll play straight into the hands of these jealous Chaldeans and give up the strategic position God's given us.* Many factors pressured them, yet they were resolute.

Why did Nebuchadnezzar bother with just three disobedient people among his myriad subjects? An egomaniac can't stand even one person who doesn't conform to his demands, let alone three.

IV. THE COERCION (DAN. 3:13–15)

A. The Report Confirmed (vv. 13–14)

"Then Nebuchadnezzar in rage and anger gave orders to bring Shadrach, Meshach and Abed-nego; then these men were brought before the king. Nebuchadnezzar responded and said to them, 'Is it true, Shadrach, Meshach and Abed-nego, that you do not serve my gods or worship the golden image that I have set up?'" Notice that he dropped the first accusation the Chaldeans made about the Jewish men not regarding the king. He knew that wasn't true.

B. The Response Commanded (v. 15)

The king gives them a second chance and repeats his command: "Now if you are ready, at the moment you hear the sound of the horn, flute, lyre, trigon, psaltery and bagpipe and all kinds of music, to fall down and worship the image that I have made, very well. But if you do not worship, you will immediately be cast into the midst of a furnace of blazing fire; and what god is there who can deliver you out of my hands?" To his credit, Nebuchadnezzar did seem somewhat just—he wanted to know if the accusation was true, and he gave them a chance to speak for themselves before he threw them into the furnace.

But Nebuchadnezzar had a short memory. He forgot that they worshiped the God who revealed his dreams and visions. Blinded by his fury, the proud king actually pitted his power against the power of God. His rage made him foolish.

V. THE COURAGE (DAN. 3:16–18)

A. Admitting Their Fault (v. 16)

"Shadrach, Meshach and Abed-nego replied to the king, 'O Nebuchadnezzar, we do not need to give you an answer concerning this matter.'"

They were respectful but not obsequious. Their answer wasn't arrogant; they simply stated that they had nothing to say. They admitted their guilt. They had faithfully served Nebuchadnezzar as far as they could, but serving his gods and worshiping his idols was beyond their allegiance.

B. Affirming Their Faith (vv. 17–18)

"If it be so, our God whom we serve is able to deliver us from the furnace of blazing fire; and He will deliver us out of your hand, O king. But even if He does not, let it be known to you, O king, that we are not going to serve your gods or worship the golden image that you have set up."

1. The expression of commitment

This is one of the greatest affirmations of faith in perhaps all of Scripture. It's easy for us to agree, from our place of comfort, but they stood on the edge of the fiery furnace. Still, the three youths offered no rationalization, compromise, or defense, but unflinchingly testified that the God they served was greater than Nebuchadnezzar. Theirs was an unwavering faith and courage. It held firm in their worst moment because they were committed to the Word of God they had been taught and therefore knew how to respond, no matter what the external pressures were. Their conviction was not dependent on whether they were delivered by a miracle. They accepted God's will even if it meant death.

2. The examples of commitment

Resist bowing to modern-day idols to gain what you desire, and present the world instead with this uncompromising spirit of integrity. Shadrach, Meshach, and Abed-nego knew that the heathen king was spiritually blind and that lengthy explanations were useless. They simply entrusted themselves to God.

a. Job

The three young men reflected the trust of Job, who declared in Job 13:15, "Though He slay me, I will hope in Him." They knew that obeying the truth of God was more important than whatever might happen to them. God is just as good when He doesn't heal as when He does, just as loving when He doesn't provide what we want as when He does, and just as gracious in His *no* as in His *yes*.

b. Paul

In Philippians 1:21 Paul says, "To live is Christ and to die is gain." The fear of death never forced Paul to compromise. He laid his head on a block, and an axe severed it from his body.

c. Martin Luther

Luther, alone as he faced his inevitable hour of excommunication at the Diet of Worms, wrote to the Elector Fredrick, "You ask me what I shall do if I am called by the emperor. I will go down if I am too sick to stand on my feet. If Caesar calls me, God calls me. If violence is used, as well it may be, I commend my cause to God. He lives and reigns who saved the three youths from the fiery furnace of the king of Babylon, and if He will not save me, my head is worth nothing compared with Christ. This is no time to think of safety. I must take care that the gospel is not brought into contempt by our fear to confess and seal our teaching with our blood" (Roland H. Bainton, *Here I Stand: A Life of Martin Luther* [New York: Abingdon, 1950], 174). Martin Luther took his cue from those three Jewish men. He didn't say, "Deliver me"; he said, "If God wants to take my life, it is a small thing."

The question was posed in Exodus 32:26, "Who is on

the Lord's side?" (KJV). Jesus said in Matthew 10:32, "Everyone who confesses Me before men, I will also confess him before My Father who is in heaven." Like those great men of God, we're to resist the pressure of the world to bow to its idols. William Cowper once wrote, "The dearest idol I have known, what e'er that idol be, help me to tear it from Thy throne and worship only Thee." No wonder John closes his marvelous epistle with the command, "Guard yourselves from idols" (1 John 5:21).

VI. THE CONSEQUENCES (DAN. 3:19–23)

A. The Fury of the King (vv. 19–20)

1. His countenance (v. 19)

   "Then Nebuchadnezzar was filled with wrath, and his facial expression was altered toward Shadrach, Meshach and Abed-nego."

   In verse 13 Nebuchadnezzar was enraged and furious, but now he was so full of wrath, it distorted his face.

2. His commands (vv. 19–20)

   a. To turn up the heat (v. 19)

      "He answered by giving orders to heat the furnace seven times more than it was usually heated."

      Though it may appear logical, Nebuchadnezzar's reaction was actually an irrational expression of anger. If he had wanted to torture the three friends, he should have turned the heat down. Heating the furnace seven times hotter would only cause instant death. In a court full of spineless flatterers and man-pleasers, the refusal of these three young men to submit to Nebuchadnezzar's immoral request caused him to lose rational control.

b. To execute the youths (v. 20)

"He commanded certain valiant warriors who were in his army to tie up Shadrach, Meshach and Abed-nego in order to cast them into the furnace of blazing fire."

The furnace was probably a pit that had an opening at the top and an opening below, where the fire was stoked. The "valiant warriors" may have been the king's personal bodyguards.

B. The Faith of the Submissive (v. 21)

"Then these men were tied up in their trousers, their coats, their caps and their other clothes, and were cast into the midst of the furnace of blazing fire."

The three young men had specially dressed for the king's ceremony. This again shows that they were not rebellious. But the king was so furious that they were hastily bound and thrown into the furnace.

God did not save them from entering the fire, He saved them in the fire. And they trusted God and were ready to suffer the experience for His glory. Perhaps they remembered the comforting words of Isaiah 43:2, "When you pass through the waters, I will be with you; and through the rivers, they will not overflow you. When you walk through the fire, you will not be scorched, nor will the flame burn you."

C. The Fate of the Strong (vv. 22–23)

"For this reason, because the king's command was urgent and the furnace had been made extremely hot, the flame of the fire slew those men who carried up Shadrach, Meshach and Abed-nego. But these three men, Shadrach, Meshach and Abed-nego, fell into the midst of the furnace of blazing fire still tied up."

The heat was so intense, it killed all the soldiers that threw the three youths in. But the young men did not burn, even once inside the furnace.

VII. THE COMPANION (DAN. 3:24–25)

"Then Nebuchadnezzar the king was astounded and stood up in haste; he said to his high officials, 'Was it not three men we cast bound into the midst of the fire?' They replied to the king, 'Certainly, O king.' He said, 'Look! I see four men loosed and walking about in the midst of the fire without harm, and the appearance of the fourth is like a son of the gods!'"

Nebuchadnezzar is jolted from his anger by astonishment. A fourth figure had appeared within the fire, and rather than lying bound, the three youths were walking around, apparently comfortable and enjoying each other's company as they patiently waited.

A. His Identity Discussed

But who was this one "like a son of the gods"? Pagan Nebuchadnezzar did not know the biblical Son of God or His Old Testament appearances, called Christophanies, as in Genesis 18. Nebuchadnezzar simply recognized that he was seeing a supernatural being; in verse 28 he refers to the figure as an angel. Whether it was Christ or an angel, he was a messenger from God.

B. His Intent Determined

God's promise to His people is consistent: "I will never desert you, nor will I ever forsake you" (Heb. 13:5). Sometimes He chooses to send angels to His people in their dire circumstances. God similarly cared for Elijah through an angel's personal service when the prophet was terribly discouraged (1 Kings 19:4–7).

How wonderful to know that we will never encounter any circumstance without God being with us. And often, the hotter the fire, the sweeter the fellowship. Peter spoke of "the Spirit of glory and of God" resting upon those who are persecuted for the name of Christ (1 Pet. 4:14).

VIII. THE COMMENDATION (DAN. 3:26–30)

A. The Rulers' Examination (vv. 26–27)

"Then Nebuchadnezzar came near to the door of
the furnace of blazing fire; he responded and said,
'Shadrach, Meshach and Abed-nego, come out, you
servants of the Most High God, and come here!'
Then Shadrach, Meshach and Abed-nego came out
of the midst of the fire. The satraps, the prefects,
the governors and the king's high officials gathered
around and saw in regard to these men that the fire
had no effect on the bodies of these men nor was
the hair of their head singed, nor were their trousers
damaged, nor had the smell of fire even come upon
them."

You know it is virtually impossible to remove
the smell of smoke from clothes, even after years.
God's miracle was evident to all, even upon close
examination: The three young men had escaped
utterly untouched by fire.

B. Nebuchadnezzar's Exultation (vv. 28–30)

1. His reasons (v. 28)

    a. The sovereignty of God

        "Nebuchadnezzar responded and said, 'Blessed
        be the God of Shadrach, Meshach and Abed-
        nego, who has sent His angel and delivered
        His servants . . .'"

Although he called their God "the Most High God" (v. 26) and proclaimed Him blessed, Nebuchadnezzar was not abandoning his polytheism; he merely ranked God highest among the many gods he worshiped. Nebuchadnezzar was expressing *henotheism*, which allows that certain peoples or nations have their own gods. He simply made room for the God of Israel as supreme over all others. This was not yet an acknowledgement of the Lord as the one true God.

b. The submissiveness of God's servants

". . . who put their trust in Him, violating the king's command, and yielded up their bodies so as not to serve or worship any god except their own God."

This sounds like Romans 12:1–2: "Present your bodies a living and holy sacrifice . . . . And do not be conformed to this world." That is exactly what they did. Nebuchadnezzar blessed the God who could elicit such allegiance. We, too, can arrest an unbelieving world by testifying to God's greatness through our own uncompromising lives.

2. His decree (vv. 29–30)

"'Therefore I make a decree that any people, nation or tongue that speaks anything offensive against the God of Shadrach, Meshach and

Abed-nego shall be torn limb from limb and their houses reduced to a rubbish heap, inasmuch as there is no other god who is able to deliver in this way.' Then the king caused Shadrach, Meshach and Abed-nego to prosper in the province of Babylon."

The three Jewish men received further promotion—if the Chaldeans were unhappy at the beginning of chapter 3, imagine how they felt now! The king decreed that anyone who disrespected the Jews' God would be cut in pieces and have their houses destroyed and desecrated. Nebuchadnezzar was determined to have this God on his side, should he ever want anything in the future. Such calculation reminds me of an NFL coach who, when asked why he always had a Christian minister on the sideline, replied that he wasn't sure he believed in God, but in case there was one, he wanted Him on his side.

CONCLUSION

You and I will probably never face a fiery furnace. But we are going to face fiery trials (1 Pet. 4:12), which can come from several sources. First of all, Satan afflicts and tempts us, as he did Jesus. Peter said that Satan is "like a roaring lion, seeking someone to devour" (5:8); he is "the accuser of our brethren" (Rev. 12:10). He wants to plant evil thoughts (Gen. 3:1–5). Satan afflicts us through the avenue of the flesh, as he did to Paul (2 Cor. 12:7). Second, the world is going to entice and intimidate us through pleasure and persecution, hoping to draw us into compromise (1 John 2:15–16; Rev. 2:10). Finally, trials are from God, to test our faith. Hebrews 12:6–8 also says that God disciplines us because we're His children.

We will all have trials. But for Christians, the end result is that we may be refined and strengthened to stand for Christ courageously and without compromise. The hymn "How Firm a Foundation" says it well:

> When through fiery trials thy pathway shall lie,
> My grace, all sufficient, shall be thy supply,
> The flame shall not hurt thee; I only design
> Thy dross to consume, and thy gold to refine.

FOCUSING ON
THE FACTS

1. In what spirit did the Chaldeans expose the Jewish men who had refused to bow to the image? Why? What part of their accusation was not true?

2. Explain what was at stake for the three friends in disobeying the king's edict—what are some factors that may have tempted them to compromise? How did most subjects of the kingdom respond? What did the Jewish youths demonstrate in their decision?

3. Sketch Nebuchadnezzar's character from this episode: What were his driving purposes? What did he think of himself? How does that relate to his rage over the few who defied his will? In what ways was he just? What was he forgetting?

4. Describe how Shadrach, Meshach, and Abed-nego responded to their enemies' charges and their enraged king. What enabled them to respond that way? How does that relate to the text's description of their clothing (v. 21)?

5. Relate the truths from Hebrews 13:5 and 1 Peter 4:14 to the three youths' experience with danger and deliverance.

6. Explain why Nebuchadnezzar's response was not indicative of saving conversion. Why *did* Nebuchadnezzar bless the God of Israel?

PONDERING THE PRINCIPLES

1. Think through some issues that are pressuring you or have pressured you in the past, either directly or indirectly. What are the consequences of compromising, from a human perspective? From a divine perspective? Realistically, are you putting God and His Word first, or do you more often compromise for some other perceived good? Explain from Scripture the importance of integrity. Prayerfully meditate on 2 Peter 1:3–7, and determine at least a few practical steps you could put into practice today to strengthen you against specific temptations to compromise.

2. According to James 1:2–3 and 1 Peter 1:6–7, what is the purpose of trials? Do you readily receive their good work in your life, no matter their nature? Examine your answer in relation to your tendency to complain about adversity generally. Consider a current or recent trial; what spiritual insights have you gained from it? How are you reflecting the attitude in Romans 5:3–4? How are you better equipped to glorify God for having gone through that particular challenge? Prayerfully meditate upon 2 Corinthians 4:8–18 to develop a proper perspective on trials, and entrust yourself to God, "who will not allow you to be tempted beyond what you are able, but with the temptation will provide the way of escape also, so that you will be able to endure it" (1 Cor. 10:13).

DANIEL IN THE
LIONS' DEN

INTRODUCTION

A. The Inevitable Mortality of Governments

Nations rise and fall with great regularity—consider the empires of the Hittites, the Egyptians, the Assyrians, and the Babylonians, followed by the Medes and the Persians, the Greeks, and the Romans. In the western hemisphere, we find tales of the great Mayan, Incan, and Aztec civilizations, but little trace of them remains besides archaeological artifacts and ruins.

More recently, we saw the greatness of France and England. Italy, under Mussolini, threatened to dominate Europe. Germany, under Hitler's Aryan philosophy, attempted to conquer the world. Japan, China, Russia, even America have all faded in their global influence today.

B. The Independent Sovereignty of God

What happens to the nations is also in God's predetermined plan (cf. Acts 17:26). But notice that His people's persistence doesn't hinge on the rise and fall of world orders. For instance, Daniel 5 records the cataclysmic fall of Babylon, and chapter 6 marks the entrance of the Medo-Persians—that second of the four empires from Nebuchadnezzar's dream in Daniel 2. At the height of its glory, Babylon, the greatest empire of its time, fell quietly to the Medo-Persians. Yet God preserved Daniel in his position as prime minister, from Babylon into the new regime.

Across America and around the world, too many Christians today are preoccupied with preserving certain nations, such as our own. They attempt to equate America with the church, or with the plan of God. But eternity, God's work, and God's plan hold the only lasting significance.

1. In Isaiah

   a. The nations as drops and dust

      Isaiah 40:15 speaks of the insignificance of nations compared to the sovereignty of God:

"Behold, the nations are like a drop from a bucket, and are regarded as a speck of dust on the scales." *Inconsequential* is the word that comes to mind. In the total history of humanity, in the flood of God's redemptive plan, one drop is inconsequential.

b. The nations as dying grass

Verses 7–8 compare the nations to grass that withers away easily. When you think back to Nimrod, Sennacherib, Nebuchadnezzar, Cyrus, Artaxerxes, Alexander, the Caesars, the pharaohs, Napoleon, Churchill, Mussolini, Hitler, Mao, Khrushchev, and so on, it is amazing to see how they and their nations come and go, yet God's work continues.

2. In Daniel

a. The reign of God

Daniel 4:17 states, "This sentence is by the decree of the angelic watchers and the decision is a command of the holy ones, in order that the living may know that the Most High is ruler over the realm of mankind, and bestows it on whom He wishes." One of our great hopes, as the people of God, is in how He makes us transcend national tumult and transition. God rules in history and is unencumbered by the decisions of men.

b. The remains of Nebuchadnezzar

Nebuchadnezzar attempted to build a lasting empire. History tells us that he put his name and titles on thousands of bricks used to build Babylon, and one writer says uncounted thousands more have been found. But ironically, one such brick was discovered with a dog's footprint over the face of the king's inscription.

So it is with the world, but God's people and plan transcend the nations' actions in history. So we see Daniel surviving in chapter 6, in the midst of the Medo-Persian Empire.

LESSON

I. THE PROMOTION (DAN. 6:1–3)

"It seemed good to Darius to appoint 120 satraps over the kingdom, that they would be in charge of the whole kingdom, and over them three commissioners (of whom Daniel was one), that these satraps might be accountable to them, and that the king might not suffer loss. Then this Daniel began distinguishing himself among the commissioners and satraps because he possessed an extraordinary spirit, and the king planned to appoint him over the entire kingdom."

A. Daniel's Superior

Because nothing about King Darius of Medo-Persia has been found outside of the Bible, we don't know for certain who he was. Some scholars posit that Darius is another name for the ruler Gubaru, whom Cyrus appointed to govern the territory of Babylon while Cyrus himself ruled the entire empire. But my preferred explanation is that Darius is another name for Cyrus.

1. His title

Archaeologists have found the word *Darius* on inscriptions for at least five different Persian rulers. It seems best to see it as a title of honor or significance, like *pharaoh*, *king*, or *Caesar*, and we can assume it was a title for Cyrus.

Verse 28 lends some help toward that interpretation: "So this Daniel enjoyed success in the reign of Darius and [or "even," in the Aramaic] in the reign of Cyrus the Persian."

2. His territory

Darius appointed "120 satraps over the kingdom" (v. 1), "and over them three commissioners" (v. 2). Obviously, he was more than a mere regional ruler in Babylon.

3. His traits

Darius, as was the historical Cyrus, was a capable,

intelligent, powerful man and an effective organizer and administrator. Though he was not committed to the true God, he did indicate great interest in Daniel's God, which only increased through the incident this chapter records.

B. Daniel's Special Abilities

Verse 2 says, "And over [the 120 satraps] three commissioners (of whom Daniel was one)." It is equally legitimate to translate "one" here as "first," which would mean Daniel was the first one chosen or the first in rank. The text makes the important point that "Daniel began distinguishing himself among the commissioners and satraps because he possessed an extraordinary spirit" (v. 3). The phrase "began distinguishing" in its original Aramaic communicates that Daniel was constantly distinguishing himself over the others.

1. Daniel was the finest statesman in the greatest world empires of his day.

2. "Excellent spirit" (NKJV) refers to his right attitude.

3. Daniel had practical experience, including:

   a. Superior wisdom

   b. A sense of history

   c. Dramatic leadership ability evidenced by the model he set for his three friends (Dan. 1)

d. Administrative skill

e. Insight into the future through his ability to interpret dreams and receive visions

C. Daniel's Strategic Appointment

God allowed Darius to recognize Daniel's capabilities and put him in a strategic position. In just the first year of his reign, the king issued a decree that the Jews return to Judah after seventy years of Babylonian captivity (Ezra 1:1–3). I believe Daniel's wisdom and influence were the cause for that decree. Although he was nearly ninety by Daniel chapter 6, he was still God's man and still the king's choice for prime minister. There is power in a virtuous life that extends into old age.

II. THE PLOT (DAN. 6:4–9)

Certain difficulty accompanies a man's exaltation to prominence. There is always the price of his devotion to his labor—he slaves at his assignment, pours his life into it. Alongside that is others' inevitable envy. Philippians 1 records that critical spirit: Some were adding affliction to Paul's bonds in prison by saying evil things about his ministry (vv. 15–17). Many hearts burn in rage, jealousy, and bitterness against another's promotion, even when that other has done them no wrong.

A. The Conspiracy (v. 4)

"Then the commissioners and satraps began trying

to find a ground of accusation against Daniel in regard to government affairs; but they could find no ground of accusation or evidence of corruption, inasmuch as he was faithful, and no negligence or corruption was to be found in him."

Intensely jealous of Daniel, his enemies sought his downfall. That they could find nothing against someone who had served publicly for as long as Daniel had testifies to Daniel's great integrity, honesty, and purity. They could discover "no negligence or corruption" in him. They found nothing that he did that he shouldn't have (a sin of commission), nor that he didn't do that he should have (a sin of omission).

B. The Conclusion (v. 5)

"Then these men said, 'We will not find any ground of accusation against this Daniel unless we find it against him with regard to the law of his God.'"

When people are unable to condemn you for anything but being sold out for God, then you are fulfilling the New Testament principle of suffering for righteousness' sake (Matt. 5:10–12). What an unintentional commendation from Daniel's enemies!

C. The Consultation (vv. 6–7)

"Then these commissioners and satraps came by agreement to the king and spoke to him as follows:

'King Darius, live forever! All the commissioners of the kingdom, the prefects and the satraps, the high officials and the governors have consulted together that the king should establish a statute and enforce an injunction that anyone who makes a petition to any god or man besides you, O king, for thirty days, shall be cast into the lions' den.'"

The Aramaic implies that the officials came together hastily and tumultuously (v. 6). Certainly Daniel wasn't consulted about this "statute and . . . injunction," which they wanted to be as binding as possible.

We know other historical monarchs who claimed to be gods: the pharaohs, the Caesars, the Ptolemies, the Seleucids. Darius was flattered. When the whole body politic wants to exalt you as a god, it's tough to resist.

D. The Commitment (vv. 8–9)

"'Now, O king, establish the injunction and sign the document so that it may not be changed, according to the law of the Medes and Persians, which may not be revoked.' Therefore King Darius signed the document, that is, the injunction."

In the Medo-Persian system, laws were unalterable and irrevocable, so they were careful about making them. But when the political leaders appealed to the king's ego, they succeeded at passing this law: If you petitioned any god but Darius for thirty days, you would go to the lions' den.

III. THE PERSEVERANCE (DAN. 6:10–11)

"Now when Daniel knew that the document was signed, he entered his house (now in his roof chamber he had windows open toward Jerusalem); and he continued kneeling on his knees three times a day, praying and giving thanks before his God, as he had been doing previously. Then these men came by agreement and found Daniel making petition and supplication before his God."

A. The Established Pattern

Despite the new law, Daniel continued to follow the pattern David had established: "Evening and morning and at noon I will pray" (Ps. 55:17, NKJV). Roof chambers in that time were often places of retreat and often had latticework over the windows for ventilation in the hot climate. So Daniel would have been visible as he faced Jerusalem and prayed for its restoration.

B. The Established Priority

When man's laws violate God's, we must give the response Peter did in Acts 5:29: "We must obey God rather than men."

Couldn't Daniel have shown some self-preservation—closing the shutters or otherwise disguising his practice? Yes, but it wasn't in his character to compromise by being self-serving.

POLYCARP'S PERSEVERANCE UNDER PERSECUTION

When Polycarp, the bishop of Smyrna and disciple of the apostle John, was burned at the stake around AD 155, his executioners called on him to deny the Lord to save his life. He answered, "Eighty and six years have I served him, and he never once wronged me; how then shall I blaspheme my King, who hath saved me?" (*Fox's Book of Martyrs*, ed. William Byron Forbrush [Philadelphia: Universal Book and Bible House, 1926], 9).

IV. THE PROSECUTION (DAN. 6:12–14)

A. The Accusation of Daniel (vv. 12–13)

1. The violation clarified (v. 12)

Now the plot thickens: "Then they approached and spoke before the king about the king's injunction." Daniel's enemies likely had the decree signed in the morning, spied out Daniel at noon, and then rushed back to report the infraction.

They asked, "'Did you not sign an injunction

that any man who makes a petition to any god or man besides you, O king, for thirty days, is to be cast into the lions' den?' The king replied, 'The statement is true, according to the law of the Medes and Persians, which may not be revoked.'"

2. The violator identified (v. 13)

Now Daniel's enemies accused him directly: "Then they answered and spoke before the king, 'Daniel, who is one of the exiles from Judah, pays no attention to you, O king, or to the injunction which you signed, but keeps making his petition three times a day.'"

Their disdain for Daniel as a subjugated foreigner is evident. And their characterization of him was untrue—he was loyal and faithful to the king as far as he could be without violating the greater King's command. He properly understood God's principles of authority (cf. Matt. 22:21).

B. The Attempt at Deliverance (v. 14)

"Then, as soon as the king heard this statement, he was deeply distressed and set his mind on delivering Daniel; and even until sunset he kept exerting himself to rescue him."

The king went from self-styled god to fool in one day. He had until evening to find an acquittal for Daniel since by their customs, executions had to occur before nightfall. Darius exhausted every legal means trying to save Daniel. But there was no way out.

C. The Absence of Defense

Daniel never said a word to defend himself. Like Christ, he was silent before his shearers (Isa. 53:7; cf. Acts 8:32–35), entrusting himself to God.

V. THE PENALTY (DAN. 6:15–17)

A. The Implementation of Darius's Law (vv. 15–16*a*)

"Then these men came by agreement to the king and said to the king, 'Recognize, O king, that it is a law of the Medes and Persians that no injunction or statute which the king establishes may be changed.' Then the king gave orders, and Daniel was brought in and cast into the lions' den."

Daniel's enemies legally subjected the king to their will.

1. The lions' plurality

These lions were purposely starved, to perform executions. We don't know how many lions were in the den, but the end of the chapter indicates there must have been many.

2. The lions' pit

The lions' den was most likely an enlarged cave in a hillside. A stone covered the mouth of the den (v. 17), and above the cave was another opening covered with a grate. The reason many believe the den was underground is that the Aramaic word for den, *gob*, is related to the Hebrew word *geb*, meaning "to dig [a pit]." The cave's natural side entrance would have been for bringing in lions and other maintenance, the top opening for ventilation and viewing executions.

B. The Impact of Daniel's Life (vv. 16b–17)

"The king spoke and said to Daniel, 'Your God whom you constantly serve will Himself deliver you'" (v. 16). Where would the king have gotten that idea? Daniel had already been serving in his court for one to two years; he would have made clear what he believed. Darius certainly heard about God and the history of His work from Daniel, and the king would have known of Shadrach, Meshach, and Abed-nego's deliverance from the fiery furnace. The king's response was fruit of Daniel's evangelistic efforts.

Still, the penalty had to be carried out: "A stone was brought and laid over the mouth of the den; and the king sealed it with his own signet ring and with the signet rings of his nobles, so that nothing would be changed in regard to Daniel" (v. 17). Nobody could break that double seal.

VI. THE PRESERVATION (DAN. 6:18–23)

A. Darius's Anxiety (vv. 18–20)

"Then the king went off to his palace and spent the night fasting, and no entertainment was brought before him; and his sleep fled from him" (v. 18). Throwing Daniel in the lions' den is the climax of the story; why cut to the king's palace? We get an insight into his deep concern for Daniel's welfare.

"Then the king arose at dawn, at the break of day, and went in haste to the lions' den" (v. 19). Darius evidently also had some faith in Daniel's God, although he may simply have been hoping for the best but believing the worst.

"When he had come near the den to Daniel, he cried out with a troubled voice. The king spoke and said to Daniel, 'Daniel, servant of the living God, has your God, whom you constantly serve, been able to deliver you from the lions?'" (v. 20). Having learned from Daniel himself that Daniel was a "servant of the living God," Darius brings us to the crux of the matter: Was God able to deliver His servant?

B. Daniel's Answer (vv. 21–23)

1. The verification (vv. 21–22)

"Then Daniel spoke to the king, 'O king, live forever! My God sent His angel and shut the lions' mouths . . .'"

The angel took care of the lions' paws too, otherwise they would have ripped Daniel to shreds. A single angel slew 185,000 Assyrian warriors (2 Kings 19:35); one angel would certainly be enough to preserve Daniel's life from lions.

2. The vindication (vv. 22–23)

a. Reported (v. 22)

". . . and they have not harmed me, inasmuch as I was found innocent before Him; and also toward you, O king, I have committed no crime."

Those statements were not expressions of pride; they were simply true. And notice, Daniel entrusted himself to God and spoke no word in his own defense until after the fact.

b. Realized (v. 23)

"Then the king was very pleased and gave orders for Daniel to be taken up out of the den. So Daniel was taken up out of the den and no injury whatever was found on him, because he had trusted in his God."

Ropes were probably lowered into the pit to pull up this nearly ninety-year-old man. Such a deliverance was God's vindication and honoring of Daniel's great faith.

It doesn't always happen that way. The prophet Isaiah was sawn in half. The apostle Paul was beheaded. Peter was crucified upside down. Believing God doesn't mean the lions will not devour you—throughout history, the faithful have been martyred. The issue is that we accept God's will at every turn: If He wills that we live, we live; if He wills that we die, we die. In either case, we're never defeated. If Daniel had been eaten by lions, he would have entered the presence of God.

VII. THE PUNISHMENT (DAN. 6:24)

"The king then gave orders, and they brought those men who had maliciously accused Daniel, and they cast them, their children and their wives into the lions' den; and they had not reached the bottom of the den before the lions overpowered them and crushed all their bones."

Note that the passage doesn't allow for liberal commentators' suggestions that Daniel escaped the lions because they were old or weren't hungry. The text insistently tells of Daniel's deliverance by God's miracle. And the lions' ferocity in this horrifying scene pictures God's just retribution and vengeance. A Medo-Persian law stated that the guilt of one was to be shared by his kindred, so the plotters' families perished with them.

VIII. THE PROCLAMATION (DAN. 6:25–27)

A. The Servant of God (vv. 25–26)

"Then Darius the king wrote to all the peoples, nations and men of every language who were living in all the land: 'May your peace abound!

I make a decree that in all the dominion of my kingdom men are to fear and tremble before the God of Daniel . . .'"

The greatest pagan empire of its day was commanded to fear the God of Daniel. God doesn't require masses to accomplish His will; He affected that entire empire through the steadfast faithfulness of one man.

B. The Sovereignty of God (v. 26)

". . . for He is the living God and enduring forever, and His kingdom is one which will not be destroyed, and His dominion will be forever."

This pagan king sounds like the psalmist! Nations come and go, but God continues strategically placing His servants and ensuring the success of His message.

C. The Salvation of God (v. 27)

"He delivers and rescues and performs signs and wonders in heaven and on earth, who has also delivered Daniel from the power of the lions."

The constant thread through this chapter—through all the book of Daniel—is not Daniel himself; it is the glory and majesty of God. The Lord stands against the backdrop of the nations of the world and upholds His sovereignty.

IX. THE PROSPERITY (DAN. 6:28)

"So this Daniel enjoyed success in the reign of Darius and [or "even"] in the reign of Cyrus the Persian."

CONCLUSION

What made Daniel so effective? As we look at this chapter and the book's early chapters, we saw Daniel first as a godly young man, and then about seventy years later still living out the same integrity. What elements of his uncompromising character could we individually apply in our own lives? Let's rapidly run through some:

1. His greatness and usefulness to God came from his perspective on history—Daniel pulled his feet out of the muck of human issues and sought the kingdom of God.

2. Tragically, most of us wax and wane in our virtue through the years, but Daniel lived with consistent virtue from start to finish. There is no simple way to measure the power of such a life.

3. He fulfilled his calling. He lived in the absolute center of God's will; his only desire was that God's will be done.

4. He had the right attitude. The testimony of him is of his "extraordinary spirit" (Dan. 6:3).

5. Though envied and hated by the world around him,

he was never embittered by it.

6. He was righteous. He was as an elder of a church should be—above reproach (1 Tim. 3:2).

7. He was known for his virtue and integrity, even among his enemies.

8. He was a faithful citizen. He abided by the law of the land and went against it only when it clearly violated the laws of God.

9. He was willing to face any consequence within the framework of God's will and leave the outcome to God.

10. He served faithfully no matter what it cost him personally.

11. He never defended himself; he left that to God.

12. He strengthened the faith of others by giving them hope in God. Even the king believed because of Daniel's great faith.

13. He entrusted himself to the will and purpose of God, even regarding deliverance from immediate harm.

14. He was a vehicle for God's glory, which is precisely what all believers are to be.

15. He did not retaliate, but trusted God to deal with his enemies.

16. Though he was exalted by those around him and

ultimately by God, he never vaunted himself.

Daniel was a real man whose life vividly illustrated the real greatness of God. And God calls Christians to follow the pattern that Daniel lived from his youth to old age—a pattern of honesty, integrity, and virtue. May we, like him, entrust ourselves to the faithful keeping of our gracious Creator, that we may be useful to Him and His kingdom in this world.

FOCUSING ON
THE FACTS

1. How does Daniel's life illustrate the persistence of God's people? How does God view world powers (cf. Isa. 40:7–8, 15)?

2. How and why did the conspirators attempt to bring Daniel down? Sketch Daniel's character—what was the only charge his enemies could level against him?

3. Why did Darius pass the decree? Explain from Scripture why Daniel disobeyed it.

4. How did the king attempt to compensate for his foolishness? How did the conspirators force his hand? Explain why Daniel did not defend himself.

5. How did Darius, a pagan, come to express belief that God would deliver Daniel? What in the passage necessitates seeing Daniel's deliverance as a miracle? How did Daniel respond to that deliverance?

6. What key issue of faith does the book of Daniel highlight? What is the book's main theme? Identify some key moments where that theme is evident.

PONDERING THE PRINCIPLES

1. Evaluate your attitudes. Do you find yourself complaining about the way things are and how they should have been, whether that be the cost of living, how your workplace is run, or on the political scene? Do you dwell on the obstacle rather than its solution? Read the following verses: Proverbs 12:25; 15:15; Romans 12:9–12; Philippians 2:1–4; 13–15. Do you allow your attitudes to depend on circumstances, or do you decide to have "an extraordinary spirit" (Dan. 6:3), no matter what? Despite his own persecution and imprisonment (see Phil. 1), what truth did Paul record in Philippians 2:13 that helps you accept your every situation with a right spirit? What is the purpose of maintaining such an attitude (vv. 14–15)? Commit yourself to showing forth the beauty of Christ by encouraging others today in the truth, regardless of your own pressures or problems.

2. How do you navigate refusing to compromise without presuming upon God's protection? Consider honestly what you would have done in Daniel's position, under Darius's thirty-day law. Even as God's Son, Jesus modeled for us how not to presume upon God, particularly regarding His protection (e.g., Matt. 4:6–7; Mark 3:7–9; John 6:15; 7:1); yet He always boldly confronted issues of God's reputation and glory (e.g. John 2:14–17; Matt. 23:13). The key question to determine a wise course of action at any

time is: Does what I'm doing serve the Lord or myself foremost? Carefully consider your recent decisions and opportunities in light of that principle.

3. Slowly look over the final list of elements which contributed to Daniel's uncompromising life. Which are characteristic of your own life? Which are you weak in? Begin praying for God's grace to grow out of your weaknesses. Choose at least one to focus on, and begin working on it through studying Scripture, depending on the Spirit, and seeking accountability, as well as other biblical means.